MW00620509

NORTH CAROLINA
MURDER & MAYHEM

NORTH CAROLINA
MURDER & MAYHEM

RICK JACKSON

THE
History
PRESS

Published by The History Press
Charleston, SC
www.historypress.com

Copyright © 2019 by Rick Jackson
All rights reserved

First published 2019

Manufactured in the United States

ISBN 9781467143561

Library of Congress Control Number: 2019945086

Notice: The information in this book is true and complete to the best of our knowledge. It is offered without guarantee on the part of the author or The History Press. The author and The History Press disclaim all liability in connection with the use of this book.

All rights reserved. No part of this book may be reproduced or transmitted in any form whatsoever without prior written permission from the publisher except in the case of brief quotations embodied in critical articles and reviews.

To my wife, Meghan, who for the past twenty years has made me strive to be a better man every day.

Also, to my children, Savannah, Ricky and Charlotte, who have given me so much happiness and purpose in life that I can never thank them enough.

CONTENTS

ACKNOWLEDGEMENTS

I would like to thank William Jackson, who was an incredible resource for me while compiling research for this book. His knowledge of law enforcement tactics, investigation methods and researching case files was invaluable. Also, thank you to Jodi Glusco from WRAL News and Dr. Maurice Godwin for providing pictures and information that have made this book more interesting. The wonderful staff of the North Carolina State Archives in Raleigh deserves thanks for teaching me so much about research during the course of writing this book.

Several people deserve thanks for the pictures and illustrations that have helped to bring this work to life. Steve Msasra and Danny Webb were indispensable in helping to organize and enhance the images found in *North Carolina Murder and Mayhem*, and a special thanks is owed to Anna Grace Hand for providing the stunning original artwork that has added a wonderful dimension to the book.

I want to thank all of the friends, family and coworkers who have given me feedback on parts of this book over this past year. Mostly, I want to thank my wife, Meghan, for the countless hours of proofreading, editing and babysitting that have gone into helping me complete this project.

INTRODUCTION

T here are few places in the world that match the beauty and majesty of the great state of North Carolina. Coming from the perspective of a native Tar Heel, that might sound like a very biased statement, and it is, but the Old North State has become a magnet for transplants in the past thirty years. It is getting harder and harder to find other natives like myself when I meet new people here. Most people, especially in a city like Raleigh or Charlotte, will tell you they moved here in 1990 something for work or because their parents moved here to take a job, and they now consider themselves North Carolinians. So, there must be something in the pine forests and kudzu-lined highways of North Carolina that calls out to strangers and says, "Come home." It truly is a special place where all are welcome.

North Carolina is flanked on its west side by gorgeous mountains and on the east by some of the finest beaches in the United States. At the center of the state is the Piedmont region, where you are only hours from either destination. The economy has always somehow missed out on the worst parts of the dark days in United States financial history. After the Civil War, during the Reconstruction period, North Carolina was home to the Duke family, who brought to the nation bright leaf tobacco and kept the farmers and manufacturers of the state busy. Universities popped up around the state, and in the Triangle area of Durham, Raleigh and Chapel Hill, there arose the Research Triangle Park (RTP). The RTP was just beginning to boom when the tobacco industry began to fall, and again North Carolina was able to avoid economic ruin by reinventing itself as a hub of technology and medical research.

Today, North Carolina offers a good economy, a mild environment, good schools and in general a nice place to raise your family. But there is a dark side to the Tar Heel State, just like anywhere else. It has not been immune to the evils of man throughout its existence. Crime has been a part of the landscape, just like it is everywhere you go, unfortunately. Even though North Carolina might not be as big or get as much coverage by the national media as some places, there have been several instances where we have taken the spotlight of the nation. There have been murders, shootings, riots and protests that have made the nightly national news.

Some have not been embedded in the national consciousness but have greatly affected the communities that they happened in and have had lasting effects on the people involved. Murder stands apart from other crimes in its severity and finality. When it hits close to home, it affects people in different ways—all bad. I have personally been in the orbit and experienced the loss of someone close at the hands of a killer more than once. It stays with you in a powerful way. It is hard to comprehend that someone can be gone forever just because someone else decides it should be so. The fact that humans have that much power over life and death is a heavy realization. Murder seems so far from normal human behavior that it changes forever the way you are able to look at people and always leaves the thought in your mind of what people are capable of doing.

I came to an understanding of what murder was when I was just a small child. My dad had been laid off from the Burlington Industries cotton mill in Durham, North Carolina, and was out of work. He had worked there as his father had and his father's father before him. The mill was all that our family had known for generations, and when it closed, he took it hard. It was a tough time for my family, and my dad was just hoping for anything when he came across an ad in the *Durham Herald* for a maintenance technician with the state at the very new North Carolina School of Science and Mathematics (NCSSM). NCSSM was a school for academically gifted high school students and was operated out of the facilities that had once been Watts Hospital, which had closed some years before. He applied and hoped for the best. He tells the story of heading out of the house to continue his job search when he heard the phone ring. He had his hand on the doorknob but stopped in his tracks, and something just told him that this was it. He turned and picked up the ringing receiver. On the other end of the phone was a friendly voice that informed him he had gotten the job. The friendly voice was a wonderful lady named Nancy Williams who worked in the Human Resources Department. She was like an angel who was the messenger of deliverance for our family. They became friends immediately, and she even encouraged him to have my mother apply for a position as a receptionist at the school just a few years later. She did, and she got the job, giving both of my parents steady and dependable employment after several years of financial hardship.

As sunny as Nancy was, there was a dark shadow hanging over her life. Her husband, Robert Williams, was very abusive, and he would beat her and threaten her and had even held a gun to her head and threatened to kill her. She feared him, and with good reason. He had been a highway patrolman, but he had gotten fired for shooting at a car that had failed to yield to his signal to stop at a traffic check. He was unhinged and dangerous. Nancy finally got up the courage to leave him, but he remained on the periphery as a threat constantly. She always said she was sure he would kill her one day. Unfortunately, she was right.

Nancy had begun to date a man named Scotty, and on Fourth of July weekend 1991, they had gone to the beach with her parents. Upon returning to her parents' house on Oberlin Road in Raleigh, they were surprised as they got out of the car by Robert, who stepped out from the shadows and shot Scotty in the neck. He dropped, and Nancy ran into the house. Gunfire rang out as Robert pursued her. Nancy retrieved a gun inside, and they exchanged fire. Neighbors thought they were hearing early fireworks and paid the exchange little attention. Nancy's elderly parents stood in shock outside, unsure of what to do or whom to call for help. Inside the house, Nancy came up short in her gunfight with Robert. She lay dead in the bathroom shower, where she had fled for shelter. He exited the back door of the house but was surprised to find Scotty had recovered from his wound and had a pistol of his own. They exchanged fire, and this time, Robert had met more than his match. He died on the way to the hospital. Scotty was in critical condition for several days after the incident, and Nancy's parents were unharmed.

It hit my family hard. My parents loved her. I had met her several times, and it was strange to realize so early that people could be taken away so suddenly and so violently. It was a shock and a tragedy—a beautiful life ripped from this world too soon. As hard as it was for my parents, and as much as I can say that it affected me, I cannot claim that Nancy was one of the closest people in our lives. She was a friend whom my parents loved dearly, but her connection was not that of a family member. Knowing the hurt in our household for Nancy, I cannot imagine the feeling of sorrow or loss at losing a child, husband, wife, father or mother can bring. Unfortunately, this was not the last time I would know someone whose life was taken so violently. Another young life was taken out of my world during a senseless crime when I was in high school. It changed my perspective on mankind and led to a reflective nature that wonders what all of those lives that have been taken would have been like. What is the world missing by not having these people here?

This book is not designed to glorify any of these crimes but to show the tragedy that has taken place in this beautiful state. For the loved ones who lost a part of themselves and mourn still, these stories may bring back feelings from dark places that will never truly go away. If they could speak for their loved ones, I think they would say that monsters do exist, and the real ones are far scarier than the ones you see in the movies. The following stories are taken from the headlines of North Carolina's history. All of these stories have drawn attention and, in many cases, kept the attention of people for years and sometimes generations. There are different reasons for this. Some have been told and retold so many times that they have almost become like ghost stories—something you have to know if you live in a certain area. Some were so devastatingly sad and senseless that they stayed in people's consciousness long after they disappeared from the newspapers and nightly news. The families never forget, and the hurt never stops.

WESTERN NORTH CAROLINA

The western part of North Carolina is a mysterious place crowned by the Appalachian Mountains, which run along the East Coast of the United States from Maine to Alabama. The mountains are filled with legend and lore that help to accentuate the rich history of the land. Native Americans once lived free among the majestic mountains and hills. European settlers looked on them with wonder as they set out to conquer yet another frontier. Today, western North Carolina is a place where people from all over the world go to slow down and relax. Stress literally evaporates like the morning mist of the Great Smoky Mountains, leaving you feeling renewed and free. But in the nooks and crevasses of these great mountains remain memories of murder and brutality. Like the wailing of a ghost, voices scream out from the past and tell tales of murder and mayhem, sadness and pain.

The mountains of western North Carolina hold many mysteries, secrets and dangers. *Author's collection.*

Chapter 1
TOM DULA

Wilson Foster woke up and pulled on his trousers. He splashed water on his face and rubbed his eyes. Worry had been keeping him from a good sleep lately, and last night had been no different. His mind raced thinking about the future for his Laura. He knew she was in trouble, and even though the rumor was that the Dula boy was going to do right by her—as right as he could at this point—it was still a bad start to a young life. Worry consumed him with his daughter pregnant and unmarried in a small community where it seemed everyone else knew more than him. He took a long look into the small mirror that hung on the wall over the dresser with the washbasin on it—amenities left behind from his late wife, who had left him alone in this world to raise a little girl and try his best to make her into a proper lady. He wished she were still with them to help tame this wild girl he had. She would know what to say in times when he stood with his mind racing but his tongue frozen. He walked through the house and stepped out on the porch, immediately noticing the old mare was gone. She stayed tied to the tree in the front of the house, but this morning she was gone. He went back inside to Laura's room and stepped in the door. Standing there with the doorknob in his hand, he felt his heart breaking inside. "Well," he thought to himself as he looked at her dresser with drawers open, showing nothing but empty space, "my girl is gone."

Thinking that she had eloped with Dula, he went about his business around the farm that day as best as he could. He was concerned for her, but he was also concerned about what he was going to do about replacing the mare that was necessary to keep the farm running. He assumed she would be back after she was wed, and presumably after the baby was born, but that would be a while yet. Just another loss due to Tom Dula, he thought. That boy was just plain trouble.

Wilson was sitting on the porch the next afternoon smoking his pipe when he heard a horse coming around the cabin. He stood and watched as the mare appeared, trotting around the corner with no rider. He hurried over to her and took her bridle, which he immediately noticed was worn and torn. It looked to him like it had been tied, and the mare had struggled and worn it down until it broke. She was hungry, and he took her to her tree and gave her some grain and sassafras. His mind was racing. His instincts were to go after Laura, but he knew he needed help, and he knew he needed the mare. She had to eat and rest for a while.

As soon as she had eaten and gotten enough rest to be ridden, he mounted her and went off to look for Laura, stopping at each homestead and recruiting help along the way. They searched the trails and common passages with no luck. Finally, they found the remnants of the mare's bridle tied to a tree and worn ground around the tree from where she had paced around trying to get loose. She had obviously been tied here and left. They searched the area, but there was still no sign of Laura. The group of men stood in the woods as birds sang around them and the sound of squirrels running through the branches broke the silence of the collective realization that they were not far from the home of Tom Dula. They remounted their horses and rode on to the Dula place, where they found Tom Dula himself. He told the group that he had not seen Laura and that he had not had any plans of running off with her. But rumors spread, and fingers began pointing at him. They had no cause to take him to the sheriff, but they decided they needed to keep looking for Laura and keep an eye on Tom. It was not long until Tom, feeling the growing pressure of rumors declaring his involvement in her disappearance, lit out for Tennessee to escape the accusations. As he rode through the Appalachians, he wondered how he had gotten involved in such a tangled web.

Before the Civil War had begun, Tom Dula was a happy-go-lucky boy in the foothills of the Appalachian Mountains. Near Wilkesboro along the banks of the Yadkin River in Wilkes County, he played his fiddle and sparked most any gal he came across with little discrimination. He was a handsome boy and a great musician, so he had little trouble catching the eyes of the young ladies. At a young age, he caught the eye of Anne Foster, who was also seventeen and a beauty. She had married an older man named

James Melton, which was not uncommon at the time. They lived together in a three-room cabin in Wilkes County. Tom and Anne were quite the match and courted up until the war came. Some nights Tom even spent the night in the Melton cabin with Anne and James, who by all accounts knew of the relationship but did not seem to be much concerned with his wife's indiscretions. They carried on like this up until the winds of war swept Tom away to the battlefields of Virginia.

When he came back from the war, he resumed his relationship with Anne Foster Melton, even spending time with her in her house and possibly sleeping nights in her bed. James and Anne had stopped sleeping together sometime before, and James did not seem to mind. Also living in the Melton house was Anne's cousin Pauline, who was paying her keep there by helping out with housework and work around the farm. Tom began to sleep with her also, which again did not seem to bother either Anne or James. It is even rumored that many times Anne, Tom and Pauline would sleep together. What Tom and Anne did not know at the time was that Pauline had come to live with them to be closer to the doctor who was treating her for the "pock," or syphilis. This would prove to be a factor in the later investigation of the murder of Laura Foster.

Laura Foster, also Anne's cousin, was a pretty girl, although not as pretty as Anne. She had two large front teeth and a large gap in between them. She lived nearby with her father, Wilson Foster. Even though Tom was involved with both Anne and Pauline, he found the time to begin an affair with Laura, sometimes even staying with her at her father's house. So Tom was a busy fellow in 1866 after he got home from the war. He was busy and happy—until a visit to the doctor. He found out that he had syphilis, and he was furious. He told one of his friends that he was going to kill the one who had diseased him. He was mad with Laura because she was his latest conquest, but the truth was that Pauline had begun the strain of the disease that involved him, Anne, Laura and James Melton. Reporters covering the trial later would be stunned at the free love atmosphere in the backwoods of Wilkes County at the time.

After the disappearance of Laura, Tom's happy-go-lucky lifestyle came to an abrupt end. Now he was on the run in Tennessee under the name Tom Hall, working for an ex-Yankee colonel named Grayson. Pauline had been in Tennessee also. She had left about the same time as Tom, and she came back a few weeks later. One of her friends joked that she must have run off because she had helped Tom kill Laura Foster. "Yes," Pauline had said, "I and Tom Dula killed her and I ran away to Tennessee." The sheriff did not think it was funny and locked her up for accessory to murder. She soon changed her story and told them that she knew exactly what had happened and that she had nothing to do with it. She said that Tom Dula and Anne Melton had killed Laura Foster and that Anne had shown her where they buried her.

She led the sheriff to a spot deep in the woods. The horses smelled it before the riders did—the smell of rotting flesh. As they approached a clearing, it became obvious that there had been digging. Leaves and soil were moved around, and animals had obviously been trying to get to something. It didn't take them long to find it under the soil and leaves: the decomposed corpse of Laura Foster, identified by the dress she was wearing and the gap between her two front teeth. She had been stabbed to death. Just one stab of the knife to her ribs under the breast had taken her life.

Anne was arrested and was taken to Elksville for trial. Tom had been arrested already and was on the way back to Elksville at the same time. His employer had found out his identity and had led the posse right to him. Tom was sitting in a creek washing his feet when they approached, and he came with them without running or putting up a fight. He rode back to North Carolina with his hands tied behind his back and his feet tied together under the horse.

In a bombshell surprise, when it came time for the trial, Tom Dula was represented pro bono by Confederate colonel and former governor of North Carolina Zebulon Vance, the hero of the Battle of New Bern. It is not known exactly why Vance would want to represent Dula, but many speculate that it was because of Dula's service in the war to the Confederacy. Vance immediately requested, and got approved, two points. One was to have the trial moved to Statesville, and the other was to have the defendants tried separately. Both were approved, though not to the benefit of Tom Dula.

Witness after witness came to the stand and offered what would be considered circumstantial evidence at best. Each aired dirty laundry, especially Pauline, who really let it all go and told the blushing courtroom everything. Love triangles, threats and syphilis—it was all there for everyone to hear, and although there was no concrete evidence, Tom Dula was found guilty of the murder of Laura Foster. Anne Melton was acquitted of the murder; many believe it was because there was just not that much evidence but also because the people of Wilkes County did not have much taste to hang a woman.

Tom appealed on the grounds of evidence being submitted irregularly, and the verdict was thrown out. Granted a new trial, he was tried again with

Tom Dula received unexpected help from Confederate hero and former governor Zebulon Vance. *North Carolina State Archive, Raleigh, NC.*

the same result and was found guilty a second time. This verdict would prove to be his last opportunity for freedom. He was hanged on May 1, 1868. He never admitted to committing the crime or exonerated Anne Melton of being his accomplice. Tom Dula became a legend the day that he was hanged for many reasons. The most important is the fact that the murder of Laura Foster and his hanging led to the folk song "Hang Down Your Head, Tom Dooley," which was written and many years later put into the popular culture by the Kingston Trio. Also, the story has so many elements to it. Love, sex, deception and mystery are woven together in this tale. The truth is much darker than that. It really is a story of a group of young people who let promiscuity and jealously lead to a young woman's death in the foothills of the Appalachian Mountains. The truth will most likely never be fully known to anyone but Laura and the person who drove the knife into her body, taking her life long before her time should have come due.

Chapter 2
FRANKIE SILVER

Charlie had not come back from his hunting trip, and his wife was worried. Or at least that is what the eighteen-year-old bride of Charlie Silver, Frankie Silver, told her neighbors in late December 1831. To them, she was hysterical with worry that Charlie had not come back. It was just not like him to be gone for so long, and she feared something had happened to him. They responded by doing what neighbors did in 1831 and set out searching for him. Coming together as a community to help someone in need; that was the way it was in Burke County in 1831. They searched and searched but found no sign of him anywhere.

Jack Collis, a local hunter, helped look for Charlie, but he just didn't feel right about something. He had spent a lifetime in the woods and had known Charlie. He just didn't see how an experienced hunter and woodsman like Charlie Silver could vanish without a trace. One day while other neighbors were searching the woods and Frankie was away from the cabin, he went in to investigate. What he found was stunning. He pushed open the cabin door, and his eyes were immediately drawn to the fireplace. There he saw bones too big to be animal bones. He entered to investigate further and found that the ashes were greasy and smelled unlike anything he had smelled before. Under the floorboards, he found a pool of blood, and as he searched around the house, he found the severed head and torso of Charlie. Staggering back from the grisly sight, he set out to get the sheriff as fast as he could.

Charlie Silver had been the only child of Jacob and Elizabeth Silver. His mother had died during childbirth, and his father had remarried soon after,

The hanging of Frankie Silver. *Illustration by Anna Grace Hand.*

bringing him into a large family where he had several half brothers. They lived in a cabin on the mountain in Burke County, and Charlie grew up to be a handsome, tall and affable young man. He could play several musical instruments and was the life of the party. Liked by all, it seemed like he could have courted any girl around, but he had an eye for Frankie. Frankie Stewart had moved to the mountain with her mother and father, Isiah and Barbara, and brother Blackston when she was just six years old. She was a smart, pretty and charming girl, and she didn't live far from Charlie. He courted her strenuously and spent much of his time at her parents' farm.

Frankie reciprocated his affection, and soon they were married. They settled down near their parents on the mountain and set about making a life for themselves. Soon they had a baby, a little girl named Nancy whom they were both very loving and dedicated to. To all around them, they seemed like a great young couple. No one could have guessed that it would end like it did, but oftentimes there is more than meets the eye. There are several speculations about the goings-on of the night of the murder. One version paints Frankie as an abused wife who couldn't take it any longer. In 1831, there was no escape from an abusive husband and no one to turn to. Many say Frankie felt trapped, and after a night of drunken abuse, she took an axe to Charlie while he slept. Others say that Frankie was a jealous young woman who thought Charlie had been unfaithful and took his life as he slept in retribution for his wrongdoings, either real or imagined. No one will know for sure. The only other person in the cabin that night was thirteen-month-old Nancy Silver.

Frankie was arrested, along with her mother, Barbara, and brother, Blackston, who were accused of knowing or even helping with the murder. Isiah was able to secure his wife's and son's freedom, but Frankie would not be so lucky. At her trial, she pleaded her innocence, and by law in those days, she was not able to take the stand to defend herself. The evidence was staggering and not in her favor. While she pleaded with neighbors to help her find her husband, pieces of him had been burning in her fireplace. His body had been butchered like a hog in her cabin and parts carried off to outbuildings. All of this had presumably happened in front of Charlie's young daughter. The all-male jury judged her guilty, and she was sentenced to hang. She was sent to the jailhouse in Morgantown to wait for her execution. But her story was far from over.

Frankie's relatives broke her out of jail as she was waiting for word of a stay of execution from the governor. The sheriff and his posse began to look for her and finally spotted her uncle driving a wagon with Frankie walking alongside. She had cut her hair short and was wearing men's clothing. As the sheriff walked his horse up to her, he looked at her and said, "Frankie." "No sir, my name is Tommy," she replied. From the seat of the wagon, her uncle tried to help her out. "Yes sir, that's *her* name, Tommy, yes sir." The sheriff took her in to custody for the second and last time, along with many of her family members who had helped her escape. Her family members were later released, but not Frankie. She sat in jail and waited for a governor's pardon that would never come.

The sheriff grew tired of waiting to hear from the governor and decided to take Frankie out and hang her, feeling, as the old saying goes, that it's "better to ask for forgiveness than permission." Frankie had talked to no one about the night of the murder during her entire time of incarceration. Why would she have done the things she did, and did she have help? She had remained silent up until she stood on the gallows with a rope around her neck. There on the gallows, with a crowd looking on, the sheriff asked her if she had any last words. She took a breath and pursed her lips to speak when her father yelled from the crowd, "Die with it in you, Frankie," leading many to believe that she had in fact had help from her family and that he was afraid of being revealed at the last minute. Frankie kept it in her just like her father wanted, and she was hanged that day for the murder of her husband, Charlie Silver. Today, in the mountains of North Carolina, they still sing of Frankie Silver and the ghastly slaying of her man.

Chapter 3
THE DEATH OF NANCY MORGAN

Jimmy Lewis was driving from his home in the Shelton Laurel community in Madison County over to Hot Springs. It was about an hour's drive along winding mountain roads, and about halfway there, he started feeling like he needed to make a quick stop and relieve himself. The road had a pretty decent amount of traffic, enough to make him look for a place to pull off to provide him some privacy. At Tanyard Gap, he pulled down an unpaved logging trail, got out and sighed with relief as he took care of the pressing business he had been dealing with. As he was finishing up, he saw a glimpse of something strange among the oak and pine trees. He walked closer and saw that it was a gray car. He came closer and looked in the back window. To his horror, he saw a naked woman in the backseat. Her hands were tied behind her back, and she was in a kneeling position. It was obvious to him that she had been dead for some time, and he rushed back to his car and to the nearest telephone to call for help. When the sheriff's office responded, they knew immediately who the young girl was. She was Nancy Morgan, who had been missing for several days.

In 1969, Nancy Morgan was a recent college graduate from Southern Illinois University at Edwardsville. She was a very liberated young woman, and she was interested in not just getting a job and making money but making a difference. She found the opportunity with the new VISTA program, which was similar to the Peace Corps but for domestic programs. The program was a promise made by President Kennedy but was born out of Lyndon Johnson's War on Poverty. The program was

President Lyndon Johnson deployed VISTA volunteers to Appalachia in his War on Poverty, fulfilling a promise made by JFK. *Courtesy of LBJ Library, Cecil Stoughton.*

aimed at providing assistance to low-income areas in the United States, including many parts of Appalachia.

Nancy, along with six other workers, came to Madison County, North Carolina, to work with local people in need. She helped teach local children about nutrition and organized physical activities to keep them playing and active. Nancy helped organize a thrift store in the community of Shelton Laurel, where she lived in an old cabin. By all accounts, she was friendly and liked by most. There was a faction of the population of Madison County that disliked outsiders and made it known. They felt that Nancy and the others could be federal agents or informants who were there to change their way of life or to report back to the feds on moonshining in the area. Much of this kind of talk was led by the Ponder brothers. Zeno Ponder was the head of the Democratic Party in Madison County, and E.Y. Ponder was the county's former sheriff.

Clarence and Glendora Cutshall owned the cabin where Nancy lived. Mrs. Cutshall had taken an immediate liking to the young girl with freckles and auburn hair. She had a constant smile on her face and was very open and trusting of everyone—too trusting, Mrs. Cutshall often told her. Nancy often came by the small grocery store that Clarence and Glendora ran in town to make connections in the community, and Mrs. Cutshall would take the opportunity to speak with her and give her advice. She told her often that she had to be more on guard with people because even in a small community like theirs, there could be people who did not have the best of intentions and might wish her harm. Nancy did not heed her advice though and was known to give strangers rides back and forth over the mountain roads. She had never met a stranger in her life, it seemed. As she neared the end of her yearlong commitment to VISTA and prepared to leave, Mrs. Cutshall's anxiety increased as she thought of Nancy being so open and vulnerable when she went back to the city on her own.

On Sunday, June 14, 1970, Nancy took a drive to the house of another VISTA worker named Ed Walker in Bluff. She had run into him the day before at Mars Hill College, where she had taken some of the local youngsters to swim. She had borrowed the county van and driven them there to give them some reprieve from the North Carolina summer sun. She had bumped into Ed and was excited to talk to someone who had had similar experiences and to be around another like-minded person. When she told Mrs. Cutshall that she was driving out to see him, Mrs. Cutshall had advised against it. Bluff was just ten miles away as the crow flies, but it was an hour's drive over winding mountain roads that were treacherous at night. Nancy waved off her concerns and arrived at Ed's cabin around 5:30 p.m.

At Ed's cabin, she strolled around the grounds with him, looking at the old well and the garden. Two local boys came by, and Nancy cooked dinner for the four of them. After dinner, they watched the comedy *It's a Mad, Mad, Mad, Mad World* on television and then the news. After the news, the boys went home, and Nancy and Ed sat on his porch looking out into the darkness of the mountain and listening to the many insects and animals calling in the woods around them. They talked for hours about their many experiences and what they wanted to do after they left. Nancy wanted to go to nursing school in New York and maybe travel some. She had already gotten her nurse's uniform in the mail and had modeled it for friends to see how she looked. She planned on coming back to Madison after nursing school to continue to help and to have an even greater impact on the community. At about 3:30 a.m., she started back toward home. Ed watched her drive away from his front porch while smoking a cigarette. Her taillights disappeared into the mountain, and Ed Walker became the last person to see Nancy alive.

The investigation was a mess immediately, with many different organizations taking part. Because the murder took place in Madison County, the sheriff's department was there. Because it was a murder, the

State Bureau of Investigation (SBI) came out to investigate, and because she was a federal employee, the FBI came also. Because of where she was found, the U.S. Forestry Service could have claimed jurisdiction as well, but it thought better of getting involved in a murder investigation. The VISTA workers were questioned, and all leads soon went cold. Former sheriff E.Y. Ponder vowed to solve the case and ran on this promise several years later, winning back his position. By the time the next election came around in 1984, he had come no closer, it would seem to the citizens, than he had been when he was reelected. Out of nowhere, it seems, Ponder brought murder charges against Ed Walker, who had since married, become a father and moved to Florida.

Returning to Madison County for trial, Ed Walker found himself in a position that no one would envy. He was forced to defend himself against a crime he had no way of proving he did not commit. He had been at home by himself at the time of the murder, and only Nancy could account for his whereabouts after the two young men had left his house that night. Also, he had provided all of the information to the authorities that he could originally and had nothing else to offer. It seemed that he had a chance of being railroaded into a murder conviction. The witness Ponder brought forward was a known liar in the county and was a habitual criminal who was facing other charges. It was only the outstanding lawyering of Ed's court-ordered attorney and the lack of credibility of the main witness for the prosecution that brought the jury to a not-guilty verdict.

After the verdict, Ed Walker tried to return to his normal life in Florida but found it difficult to live with the dark cloud that seemed to always hang over him. Although he had been found not guilty, it was little vindication because of the stigma of the accusation. In Madison County, the trail ran cold for investigators, and they soon went back to the days before the Ed Walker trial. The authorities left the case open and followed leads, but for the most part, the evidence they had did not warrant the arrest of any other suspects, and the limited resources for the local authorities and the SBI did not make a cold case that was decades old attractive to investigators. Even a prison confession by a local known criminal was not enough to spring anyone to action to solve the murder. Unfortunately, Nancy Morgan found herself in a part of the world that was foreign to her, and although she had the best intentions to change the world and make things better for the people of Madison County, someone taking her life was her reward. There is no way to know what this young lady would have become or what good she would have done. The only thing known for sure is that her death was a senseless tragedy.

Chapter 4

THE DISAPPEARANCE OF JUDY SMITH

Newlyweds Judy and Jeffrey Smith sat in the car at Logan Airport in Boston, Massachusetts. Judy had looked everywhere, and it was apparent that she had forgotten her driver's license at home. Apologizing, she said goodbye to her husband of eight months as he headed out to catch his flight. Jeffrey had a scheduled conference in Philadelphia and had wanted Judy to come with him so he wouldn't be alone. She promised she would catch a later flight and meet up with him at the hotel. He took the flight into Philadelphia and attended the first day of the meeting. When he arrived back to the hotel, he found that sure enough, there in the lobby was Judy, smiling and holding flowers as a way of saying "I'm sorry." They grabbed a bite to eat and discussed their plans for the rest of the trip. By day, they would go their separate ways, Jeffrey to his meeting and Judy to see the sights around town. At night, they would see friends and visit tourist sights together. Despite the bad start to the trip, they were now on schedule to make it a great one.

The next morning, April 9, 1997, Jeffrey woke and went down to the lobby for breakfast. Judy was sleeping soundly, and he did not want to wake her up. When he returned, she was in the shower. He came in and chatted with her for a moment before he had to go. She was planning on going to see the Liberty Bell and Independence Hall. He had to leave for his meeting, but before he left, he told her to try the continental breakfast downstairs. Judy playfully swung back the curtain and said, "I think I'll go like this!" When Jeffrey walked out of the door, he was laughing and could hear her laughing behind him. It was the last time he would ever see or hear from her. When he got back to the hotel that night, she was gone. At first he thought she was just late getting back from her sightseeing, but as the evening progressed, he became very concerned. He had the hotel call around to local hospitals and urgent care centers. Coming up empty, Jeffrey tried the police department. It had no record of any incidents involving anyone who fit Judy's description. He tried to make a missing person's report, but officers told him he had to wait until she had been missing for twenty-four hours. He spent the rest of the night riding around Philadelphia looking for her, with no luck.

Heavy hearted, he returned alone to Boston, but he did not stop looking for Judy. He spent the next few months calling in missing person's reports to authorities across the country. He sent missing person flyers out by the thousands to police departments, hospitals and shelters, desperately hoping for some word from Judy or about her. In the days following her disappearance, there were reports of sightings in Philadelphia; in Easton, Pennsylvania; and even in New Jersey, but all of the leads came up cold. Jeffrey even hired several private investigators to search for Judy, but there was still no news, good or bad.

A few months later, in the dense woods of the Pisgah National Forest near Asheville, North Carolina, a father and son made a gruesome discovery. They were hunting deer, but what they found that day scattered on the ground by animals were human bones. The pair retreated out of the woods and alerted the closest authorities. When investigators got to the scene, they found human remains wrapped in a blue blanket that had been buried in a shallow grave. There was still a wedding ring on the finger of the remains, and the bones had been dug up and moved by wildlife. The body was dressed in hiking clothing, thermal underwear and hiking boots. Close by, they found a blue backpack buried with winter clothes in it and eighty dollars in cash. In another spot, they found a shirt and sunglasses buried. The shirt also contained eighty dollars in cash. When the medical examiner looked at the bones, he could see that it was a female around forty-five to fifty years old with an arthritic knee. There were holes and cuts in the bra and cuts on the chest bones, indicating that the woman had been stabbed to death.

A doctor at a nearby hospital saw the medical examiner's report and remembered seeing a flyer that had been sent out by Jeffrey Smith. He called in the tip, and the medical examiner then requested the dental records of Judy Smith. The medical examiner compared the records to the body that was found. They matched, and upon receiving the news, Jeffrey was heartbroken and confused about who would have done such a thing and how this could have happened. The discovery of Judy Smith's body opened a door to so many questions that no one could answer. To make the situation even more confusing for the authorities, and for Judy's family, after the news reported her as the person that had been found by the hunters, people began to report that they had seen her in and around Asheville soon after the reported disappearance. Several people identified her as a customer in their business or someone they had come in contact with. By all accounts, she was alone and very friendly. No one considered her to be in any duress or anything other than a very nice tourist. The police ruled out Jeffrey as a suspect immediately. He had an airtight alibi when she went missing, and the place in the woods where they found her would have been too hard for him to get to because he was very overweight. Even if he had been able to secretly get away from everyone unnoticed and travel over six hundred miles to Asheville, it would have been almost impossible for him to get her body to the location where it was found. There were just no leads and no rhyme or reason for her to be in Asheville.

There are many theories about Judy's disappearance, but none seem plausible. Many have speculated that she wanted some time away from her husband and snuck away from Philadelphia to travel and have time to herself. All of her family and Jeffrey's have come forward to say what a great marriage they had, and it begs the question, if she wanted time to herself, why not just stay in Boston while he was away for the week? Others have theorized that she had a secret life of some kind that she had been hiding from everyone and had traveled with another man to Asheville to run away. But again, it seems more logical that she would have just spent the time in Boston to do this since her husband was going to be out of the picture for some time anyway. Another point of contention is how she got from Philadelphia to Asheville. If she had taken public transportation or rented a car, someone would have seen her, or there would have been some form of record for her travel.

However it happened, the fact that she somehow found herself hiking in the Pisgah National Forest is certain. Her family recognized none of the clothes they found her in or the bag or sunglasses. She had not been robbed of any of her valuables; they had been buried with her in the shallow grave in the forest. Some have pointed the finger at a monster who did not reveal himself until a decade later when, in the same area, he beat an elderly woman, Irene Bryant, to death and shot her husband, John. Gary Michael Hilton was a drifter and moved around a lot in his life. He was a lover of nature and often took his dog with him on walks along hiking trails. It was here he met his victims. After killing the Bryants, he moved on to Florida and Georgia, killing again in both states in national forests. He was caught in Georgia and sentenced to life at seventy-one years old. Most experts believe it is implausible that he would have begun killing at this advanced age and consider it a possibility that he was the murderer of Judy Smith as well. If he killed her, he has never confessed to the crime.

The death of Judy Smith was a tragedy, as all murders are. Many times when someone goes missing, loved ones just want to know. Especially when it comes to the point when they know they are not coming back, they want to know what happened to receive some form of closure, some way to stifle the pain of having their imaginations run wild for the rest of their lives. When Judy was found, only one question was answered: Is she alive? Unfortunately for the family, it created hundreds of other questions that will most likely never be answered. There is no evidence and nothing for any investigators to pursue. Unless someone decides that getting her murder off their conscience will somehow relieve some guilt for them, there will probably never be any answers.

Chapter 5

MURDERS IN THE STORM

The wind was howling and at times shaking the side of the trailer. Cecil Small was in for the night for sure. It had started snowing around 3:00 p.m. that afternoon of Thursday, February 3, 1972, and the storm had increased steadily. Now it was after 10:00 p.m., and the wind was blowing hard and the snow was still falling. There was not much that could get him to venture out into the mess swirling around his little trailer. About 10:30 p.m., a banging on his door startled him. Cecil rose from his chair and went to the door. Looking through the curtains, he could see his neighbor Troy Hall bundled up in the snow with his arms wrapped around his body and swaying from side to side in the storm. Cecil opened the door and brought him inside, asking if everything was all right as Troy entered the room and pulled down the hood from his coat.

He told Cecil Small that he had gotten home from school at Appalachian State and was listening to music with his wife, Ginny, when the phone rang. He told him the voice was muffled and hard to understand, but he heard his mother-in-law, Virginia Durham, say that "three niggers" were holding them in the house and were beating her husband and son in another room. The phone went dead. He had tried to call back, but the line was busy. Troy told Cecil that he thought it must have been his mother-in-law trying to make a prank call to get them going but the line had gone out before she could tell him it was a joke. He was planning on brushing it off, but Ginny had become concerned because they were not able to get in touch with them, and she wanted him to drive her over to their house, about four miles away.

The problem was, when he had gone outside to start the car, the battery was dead. This seemed to agitate Ginny more, and long story short, Troy told Cecil he was wondering if he could drive them to the Durham house to check on his in-laws. Not much could have gotten Cecil Small outside that night, but a neighbor in need was one of those things.

They drove through the snow, taking their time, and arrived at the Durham house to find the driveway iced over. Cecil tried to drive up the steep driveway, but it was useless. He parked his car at the bottom of the drive, and he and Troy left Ginny in the car and proceeded to the house on foot. They knocked, but no one answered. Lacking a key to the house, Troy lifted the garage door enough for the two of them to crawl under and enter the house. As they walked from the garage into the dwelling, it was obvious something was very wrong. The house had been ransacked, and things were thrown all around. They proceeded with caution, and as they came upon the bathroom, they could see through the open door the bodies of the Durham family, Bryce, Virginia and Bobby Joe, with their hands bound behind their backs and their heads bobbing in water in the bathtub. The three were obviously dead. The two men looked at each other and made a hasty retreat out of the house, down the drive and to a neighbor's house to call the police.

Records show that the Boone Police Department was dispatched at 10:50 p.m. that night. Officers arrived around 11:00 p.m. and, upon entering the house, began to take account of the scene. The three victims were kneeling at the tub with their heads in the water. Later autopsies would show that Bryce and Bobby Jo had been strangled and then drowned. Virginia had died from strangulation before her face was also put in the water beside her husband's and son's. They found three glasses with Coke and food in the living room. The television was on, and there was half-eaten baked chicken in the kitchen on the counter. It was obvious they had been surprised while enjoying dinner in front of the television. A neighbor told the police that Bryce had driven home a white-and-green GMC Jimmy truck that afternoon from his Buick dealership, but it was missing. Shortly into the investigation, the State Highway Patrol called in a report of an abandoned vehicle. A green-and-white Jimmy was on the side of the road still running with the wipers going and the Durham family's silverware inside. There was very little physical evidence that would help the police solve the crime. First, they had to find out who these three unfortunate people had been.

Bryce Durham was a native of Wilkes County, North Carolina, and had moved to Mount Airy to work in the auto loan business. He did well. Bryce and his wife, Virginia, had a daughter, Ginny, and a son, Bobby Joe. Ginny was the elder and had recently married Troy Hall and moved to Boone to attend ASU with her husband. Bryce Durham, who was eager to stay close to his daughter, was able to move from Mount Airy with his family to Boone to open Boone's Buick dealership. This was the culmination of a lifelong dream for a hardworking man. He settled into the community, and his family kept to themselves for the most part. Virginia worked at the dealership with her husband, and Bobby Joe was also accepted to Appalachian State University. The day of the murders, Virginia had called Bobby Joe and told him they were bringing him home with them that night because they had just gotten in the Jimmy, which was four-wheel drive. The three of them had driven home that night; the same neighbor who had identified the truck to the police said they had arrived home around 8:30 p.m.

By all accounts, the Durhams were just a simple, hardworking family. The police were at a disadvantage in the investigation. There was snow outside but no footprints because of the volume of snow coming down, along with the treacherous wind that was blowing that night. No prints could be found except those of the family members in the house. The house had been ransacked, but why? If the motive was robbery, then the thieves had missed several valuables, including a bag of cash in view on a kitchen chair. Also, the silverware that was taken had been abandoned with the car. Officers really had no leads despite the participation in the investigation of several local departments, as well as the North Carolina SBI.

There were many theories regarding the slayings. One was that the Durhams had become involved in some shady business practices through the car dealership, possibly even with drug smuggling in cars, but a review of the Durhams' finances and that of the business showed no indication of anything other than square dealings. There was a theory because of the manner in which they had been killed that professional hit men had been involved. Authorities could find no evidence of anyone who would want the family killed. One last theory was that an announced military exercise by the Green Berets in the area had gotten out of control. Many speculated that in the gear up for deployment to Vietnam, they had gotten carried away and murdered the family to hone their skills. Again, there has never been any evidence of this taking place.

Many have questioned the involvement of Troy Hall. He was last seen by anyone other than his wife that night at 8:00 p.m. at the Appalachian State University library. The call that he says he received was strange. He stated that his mother-in-law had called him and said that Bryce and Bobby Joe were being attacked in the other room, but why would she call him and not the police? Also, she identified the race of the attackers as black, but the police did not find any hairs belonging to African Americans in the entire house. It is one thing for a perpetrator to wipe prints or wear gloves, but it is very difficult for what would have to have been multiple men (three if the call is to be believed) to not lose a single hair follicle. Some of the most prominent investigators involved in the case believe the call never happened.

The case remains unsolved to this day. Troy and Ginny moved from Boone to Wilkes County soon after. They cooperated with investigators, but no motive or evidence was ever brought forward to implicate them in the murders. They divorced in 1976 and went their separate ways. Even though the case has remained open and has garnered attention from time to time, there have been no other leads or new evidence in decades. For now, the strange murders on that snowy night will remain a mystery and continue to be told of around campfires and around late-night study tables at the university.

Chapter 6
THE CAPTURE OF THE OLYMPIC BOMBER

Murphy, North Carolina, is a small town. It has never been known for much, except being the county seat of Cherokee County. Two railroad lines used to meet there, connecting Asheville and north Georgia, and briefly, Murphy had a chance of being a good-sized town. But by the 1880s, the line from north Georgia had been removed. Murphy continued to be as it is today, a little town on the westernmost tip of the state. Not much exciting has ever happened there—except for one morning in 2003 when one of the highest-profile arrests in the history of the United States took place behind a local grocery store, ending a five-year manhunt and jailing one of the FBI's ten most wanted criminals.

Early on the morning of May 31, 2003, Officer Jeff Postell was making his rounds through Murphy. He drove into the empty parking lot of the Save-A-Lot grocery store and cruised by the front doors. No glass broken, doors closed—everything was looking good. He slowly pulled around the corner of the store and proceeded around back to check everything out. As he came around the corner, he saw a thin white man behind the store moving between two dumpsters with his back to him. The man was dressed in a camouflage jacket and work boots and had something in his hand that Postell could not identify—maybe a gun. Officer Postell moved closer and opened his door, thinking he had come upon a burglary in progress. He stepped out of the patrol car and, from behind the door, pulled his gun and ordered the man to drop whatever was in his hand and get on his knees. The man complied, and Officer Postell called for backup. When other officers arrived, they took the dumpster diver into custody. He was compliant and said his name was Jerry Wilson, he was from Ohio and he was homeless. He didn't have a gun; it was a flashlight. They took him in to the station to check him out further.

Back at the police station, he was questioned, but his story was just not adding up. He was almost too compliant and too willing to tell them what they wanted to know. His story seemed contrived. Finally, an officer who had been looking at him as if he had seen him somewhere before decided to check the wanted posters they had on file. He was taken aback when he looked at the FBI poster for the Olympic bomber, Eric Rudolph. The man in custody was slimmer and more haggard looking, but it was him. The officers pressed him about his identity, and without much pushing, he soon admitted his true identity. He shrugged his shoulders and simply said, "You got me." This rookie cop on a small-town police force had just captured one of the most wanted men in the nation.

Eric Rudolph had spent his formative teenage years in North Carolina. He dropped out of school in the ninth grade and joined the army. He was trained at Fort Benning, Georgia, and served at Fort Campbell in Kentucky. He left the army in 1989 and fell deep into the Christian Identity movement, which is a racist anti-Semitic group that preaches white supremacy. He became obsessed with homosexual activity and what he saw as society's acceptance of a great sin. He especially was bothered by the abortion of unborn children and turned his attention to fighting its perpetrators. He began to consider violent opposition to abortion and homosexual activity as his moral duty and soon put his beliefs into practice.

In 1996, Atlanta was hosting the Summer Olympic Games, and there was energy and excitement running through the city. On July 27, the Atlanta Police Department received a call saying that there was a bomb planted in Centennial Olympic Park. At the park, just minutes before the police received this call, security guard Richard Jewel found a bag with three pipe bombs in it. He alerted the police also and began to move people out of the area. When the bomb went off, it killed one person and wounded one hundred others. Another man died of a heart attack while running from the scene. Jewel was initially lauded as a hero, but he quickly became a prime suspect in the court of public opinion as the news media began referring to him as a person of interest. He was eventually cleared, but not before his name was permanently ruined. These were just the first victims of Rudolph's crusade.

In January 1997, a bomb went off in Sandy Springs outside Atlanta at an abortion clinic. A month later, the Otherside Lounge, an Atlanta

Olympic Park bomber Eric Rudolph was captured in Murphy, North Carolina, going through a dumpster behind a supermarket. *Illustration by Anna Grace Hand.*

gay bar, was bombed and five people were injured. In January 1998, another abortion clinic was bombed in Birmingham, Alabama. This time, a Birmingham Police Department officer, Robert Stephenson, who worked as security there was killed and a nurse was critically injured. After the Birmingham bombing, Rudolph was identified by two men who saw him and noted his license plate number. He was soon linked to the other bombings and was named to the Ten Most Wanted List by the FBI. A week later, his truck was found in Cherokee County near where he had grown up, abandoned with no signs or clues about where he might have gone.

Rudolph seemed to disappear off the face of the earth. Even the million-dollar reward offered for his arrest was not enough to bring him to justice. Authorities felt that he was in the area of Cherokee County and searched the forests of the national parks nearby but came up empty-handed many times. Rudolph related after his arrest that he had gone into the wild when he began to feel the pressure from law enforcement after the Birmingham bombing. He had lived off the land for the most part, collecting berries and eating lizards at times. He often snuck into Murphy at night and prowled the dumpsters of restaurants for discarded food. He watched from afar and learned when to forage—when stores got deliveries that were unattended long enough to pillage, which mountain cabins were unused and when he could use them. During the cold mountain winters, he would break into the unused cabins to stay warm. He had buried fifty-five-gallon drums in the ground and at night would sneak into a local granary and steal a small amount of grain or soy and fill up the drums for food later.

Rudolph was a true survivalist, and because of his minimalistic abilities, he was able to evade the law for years. He depended on his skills and a great deal of luck, and on that early morning in May, his luck ran out. Rudolph was able to strike a plea deal with the government to save his life by telling them the location of 250 pounds of dynamite that he had buried for later bombings. He will live out his life in federal prison. He has written many letters and even had his memoirs published from prison. Legal battles

Dynamite seized by the FBI after the capture of Eric Rudolph. *Courtesy of the FBI.*

have followed about how to deal with what many people feel is hate speech coming from prison. The court has ordered that any money made from the sale of the memoirs be paid to victims as restitution, but little can be done to assuage the grief that is felt over lost loved ones. Nothing can be done to restore those lives, and although Eric Rudolph will spend the rest of his life in prison, he will still be able to enjoy many of the things that he took from so many other people

Chapter 7

THE SHELTON LAUREL MASSACRE

The American Civil War tore the United States apart and pitted neighbors against each other. Brother fought against brother on battlefields across the young nation, and loyalties were tested. North Carolina contributed greatly to the Confederate cause. Even though there had been trepidation among North Carolinians leading up to secession, there was a high degree of patriotism in the Piedmont and eastern part of the state toward the Confederacy. That was not the case in the mountains of the Tar Heel State. There were no plantations and very few slaves in western North Carolina. The citizens did not see the need for the institution, nor did they see the impact that slavery had on the economy of the South. Because of this, many people in the mountains saw no need for changing anything since they would not be affected either with the abolition of slavery or the expansion of it. Also, the population of the mountain region existed more in a clannish environment where family lineage was more important than government. What flag flew over government buildings was of little concern to people who followed laws older than that of any government. Being left alone, more than anything, was the desire of those in the mountains.

The mountains, to a great extent, stayed loyal to the Union for this reason, seeing no reason to change and certainly no reason to fight and die for change. When open hostilities began, many young men headed north to join the Union army. Others stayed and tried to remain neutral or act as agents providing any information they could to the North. When the Confederacy enacted the Conscription Act of 1862, families found themselves in a situation where they could not remain on the sidelines any longer. Men from the mountains who were forced into service looked for the first opportunity to run off and head back home in many cases. In Madison County, many of the deserters who came back became guerrillas and bushwhackers, harassing the Confederates at every opportunity. The Union command saw an opportunity to cause chaos behind the Confederate lines, so it dispatched Colonel George Kirk, a Confederate deserter himself, to command the Unionist force in Madison County.

On January 8, 1863, the bushwhackers raided the town of Marshall, where there was supposed to be a supply of salt. The raiders were convinced that the Confederates were trying to starve the local Union-loyal population over the winter by withholding salt from the people of the county, but as with most resources during war, it is more likely they were withholding the salt to cure meat for the army. When the raiders struck, they did not just attack the salt reserve. They attacked the town and looted the stores and houses there also. Clothes, shoes and valuables were taken. The raiders broke into the home of Confederate colonel Lawrence Allen of the Sixty-Fourth North Carolina and stole valuables and harassed his family. His children were ill with scarlet fever and died shortly after the raid. This raid would be the tinder that was needed to send Madison County over the edge and into a violence that exceeded even what had been experienced on the battlefield.

When news of the raid reached Colonel Allen, he was furious. He was too ill to travel himself, but his second in command, Lieutenant Colonel James Keith, led the Sixty-Fourth onto the Shelton Laurel Valley in Madison County with revenge on their minds. The Sixty-Fourth was a veteran group of fighters, and they pursued those they felt responsible throughout the valley, skirmishing with some pro-Union forces and killing over a dozen men. When the governor of North Carolina, Zebulon Vance, was informed of the ride the Sixty-Fourth was making through the valley, he ordered that the captured looters not be harmed. Vance was from the area and understood the underlying feelings on both sides and did not want to see Madison County turn into a killing ground. He dispatched North Carolina attorney general Augustus Merrimon to the area to monitor the situation and report back to him.

When Allen finally joined Keith, they disregarded the governor's orders. Vengeance was on Allen's mind after burying his children, and he was convinced that the locals knew who the bushwhackers were but that they would not just offer up this information without coercion. They began rounding up women in the valley who they thought could provide information. Several women, some as old as eighty-five, were whipped with hickory rods until they bled. Several were taken to trees and had nooses secured around their necks. Soldiers would raise them up with their feet just off the ground and let them strangle until they almost died. Then they would lower them again to see if their memories had improved. The Confederates burned houses and killed livestock in the valley, but the men who had raided Marshall were still not found or coaxed out of hiding. The Confederates rounded up the people they thought were supporters of the bushwhackers and began the long march back to the Confederate stronghold of East Tennessee, where they would be held as prisoners.

They did not get far. Two men escaped and disappeared into the immense woods that surrounded the valley. A furious Keith ordered the rest of the prisoners be taken off the trail and into the woods. There, he had five of the prisoners lined up, among them boys as young as thirteen and fourteen. Hands tied behind their backs, they stood facing a line of soldiers with rifles ready. The order was given to take aim at the prisoners. The soldiers nervously took their firing positions, wondering if Colonel Keith could really be serious. The oldest man in the group of prisoners looked around him at the soldiers and the other prisoners and said, "For God's sake men, you are not going to shoot us?" Silence greeted his inquiry as shaking hands held pointed rifles and Keith stood to the side of his men, glaring at the prisoners. "If you are going to murder us, give us time to pray!" he pleaded, but Keith answered, "There is no time for praying" and ordered the men to fire. They hesitated, and for a moment it seemed they would not follow his order. Furious, he glared at his men and shouted that if they did not fire then they would join the condemned. At that, fire leapt forth from the barrels of the Confederate rifles. Four of the captives fell dead instantly. The youngest of the group was not killed but crawled forward and clung to the leg of one of the soldiers, pleading for his life, but he was shot dead. The rest of the captives were murdered in the same manner as the first five and dumped in a trench in the woods.

When Merrimon learned of the murders, he was appalled. He immediately sent word back to Governor Vance, who was likewise sickened by the killings of the civilians. An investigation was ordered, and Allen was suspended from the army for six months. As the war began to go badly for the South, the matter was shelved for the duration. It was not until after the war that any other action would be taken against any of the men responsible. The two men who bore the burden for the murders were Allen and Keith. Colonel Allen was in command of the column but was not in command of the men

Letter written by A.S. Merrimon, who was tasked with investigating the Shelton Laurel Massacre, to Governor Zebulon Vance. *Courtesy of the North Carolina Museum of History.*

at the time of the execution, so the responsibility fell to Lieutenant Colonel Keith. He was tried for the murders after the war and was found guilty. After two years in prison petitioning for the Supreme Court to look at his case, he escaped and was never seen again. By a coincidence of timing, it was only a few days after his escape that the North Carolina Supreme Court issued a decision on his case; he would have been freed.

The murders were never really satisfied in the community, where the people of Madison County never felt that justice was done. In a place where family ties run deeper than patriotism and everyone knows everyone else, it created years of conflict in the county after the war was over. People remembered who was killed and who had done the killing for generations, and the massacre remains a tragic climax in what for a nation was a civil war but for a county in the mountains of North Carolina was more akin to a family feud.

Chapter 8
ON CHRISTMAS MORNING

In 1918, Charlie Lawson moved his family to Germantown, North Carolina, to work on a tobacco farm. He had been married for seven years to his wife, Fannie, and they had three children: Arthur, Marie and William, the latter of whom would die of an illness in 1920. The times were hard, but the move turned out to be a good one for the Lawson family. By 1927, Charlie could afford to buy his own farm in the area, and the family continued to grow. Charlie was known around town and the county as an honest, hardworking man. He belonged to the Germantown Lodge, and despite the fact that he was known to squabble with his wife on occasion, he was considered to be a good man and a good neighbor. By 1929, they were settled in the community and were a family of nine.

A few days before Christmas that year, Charlie loaded up his family and went into town. He bought them all new dresses and suits, and they sat for a formal portrait in the town's photography studio. This was unusual for a family like the Lawsons because it was a huge expense. Mostly the only customers that the photographer had were citizens planted firmly in the upper class of society. Fannie tried to talk Charlie out of it because it was so extravagant, but he insisted it was all part of a Christmas surprise. Charlie, Fannie (holding their newborn baby, Mary Lou), Arthur and Marie stood behind the small children, Carrie, Maybell, James and Raymond. Not a smile can be seen on anyone's face in the picture. Was it that the family was not familiar with the process of taking portraits, or was the family just in a miserable state that outsiders would not understand? No one can know for sure, but one thing that is known beyond a doubt is that Charlie indeed had a Christmas surprise in store for them all. When they finished with the portrait, they loaded back up for home. Christmas Eve was wonderful, and Charlie Lawson's family spent the night fulfilling the same family traditions they had every year—not knowing this would be their last.

Christmas morning started off as a beautiful snow-covered day in Stokes County. The frigid cold was broken by a bright sunlight that shone through the trees and offered great visibility for a hunt. Charlie took Arthur and his cousin out early to hunt rabbit, telling them that it would make for a good stew the next day. After a morning of shooting rabbits, they headed home. As they neared the Lawson homestead, Charlie told Arthur that they were out of shells and he had best head into town to get some more. The hunting had been good, and he said he wanted to make sure they had enough to go again tomorrow if the weather held up. Arthur set out with his cousin for town, unaware of what was about to take place. Not knowing that something inside his father had snapped. That there was a secret that he could not, and would not, let get out.

Back home, Carrie and Maybell kissed their mother goodbye and set out to their uncle's nearby house to visit for Christmas. They walked together, and as they approached the barn, their father stepped out from behind it. They were startled but not afraid to see their father—until he raised his shotgun and pointed it at them. They stopped in their tracks as a rush of fear and confusion spread over them. Two shots rang out, and the little girls fell where they stood. Charlie pulled their lifeless bodies inside the barn and laid them beside each other with their hands folded across their chests. He headed for the house. Fannie stood on the porch, having heard the shots. She knew the boys had been hunting and had heard several shots already, but these seemed closer. She stood on the porch with her hands on her hips as she saw Charlie walking up to the house carrying his gun.

The look on his face was not one she had ever seen before. When he came closer, she opened her mouth to ask him about the shots, but before she could speak, he leveled his shotgun and fired it into her chest. She crumpled on the porch dead. Marie had seen her mother from inside the house, and she began to scream hysterically. Charlie burst through the door and shot her down as she was screaming for her life. The two younger boys in the house ran and hid as soon as their mother was shot. Charlie walked through the house and systematically searched for the boys. His boys. He found them and shot them each, moving on to four-month-old Mary Lou, who was screaming in her crib, startled by the loud noises. He stood over her, looking down, and then took the butt of the shotgun and beat her to death in her crib.

After the killing was complete, he went through the house and laid them all out, folding their hands across their chests as he had done with the girls. He went outside and got a rock to place under each one of their heads like a pillow. He looked around at his family, and then he disappeared into the woods. Not long after Charlie ran off into the woods, his brother Elijah and his nephew Claude, who were coming to visit, came upon the body of Fannie. They backed away from the scene and rushed to town to get the police. When the bloody scene was discovered, the police and local residents swarmed the house. The last surviving member of the family, Arthur, returned from town and wept for his family. They heard another gunshot from the woods nearby and followed the sound, finding Charlie Lawson leaned against a tree, dead by his own hand. The snow was trampled down in a ring around the tree, illuminating the track Charlie had paced before his death, around and around, no doubt contemplating what he had done. In his pockets they found letters to his parents but nothing explaining why he had committed these ghastly murders.

Nobody knows why Charlie Lawson carried out such a heinous act against his family that Christmas morning. The dominant theory is that Charlie had been engaged in an incestuous relationship with his seventeen-year-old daughter, Marie, and she had become pregnant. It is thought that Fannie knew about this and Charlie feared what would happen after this secret got out. It is also noted that Charlie had sustained a head injury a few weeks before the murders, and many believe he might have suffered brain damage that affected his mental capacity. He had been digging a cellar, and the mattock he was swinging bounced back and hit him in the head. It was so bad that he went to the doctor to get checked out; however, at the time, the method for checking for brain damage was primitive, and he was sent home. Charlie walked around with two black eyes for several weeks. Many feel that the head injury changed him and caused him to be out of his mind when he committed the murders. The Lawsons were also known to fight on occasion. It seems like the community knew that the family had their share of troubles, although the exact reasons remain a mystery.

Arthur—who was sent away by his father, most likely because he would have been the only member of the family who would be able to possibly stop him—went on with his life the best he could. He married and had children but was killed in a car accident just fifteen years later. Charlie's brother Marion saw the opportunity to make money from the tragedy and

The Lawson family cabin was the site of a grisly Christmas morning surprise by family patriarch Charlie Lawson. *Private collection.*

opened up the house as a tourist attraction. He left the house just as it had been on the day of the murders and for a fee would let people come in to see the bloodstains on the floor. He even left the cake Fannie had baked that morning on the table where it had been. Over the years, people picked the raisins off the top of the cake as souvenirs of the grisly scene. The Lawson family was buried together in a family cemetery in Stokes County. Slayer lay alongside the slain forevermore under a stone inscribed, "Not now, but in the coming years, it will be a better land; We will read the meaning of our tears and then, sometime, we'll understand." Although many years have passed, no one truly does.

THE PIEDMONT

The largest and most populated region of North Carolina is the Piedmont region. Truly the heart of North Carolina, this is where you will find the largest cities, such as Charlotte, Winston-Salem and Greensboro, as well as the Triangle area composed of Chapel Hill, Durham and the state capital of Raleigh. Tobacco was king here once, and textile mills sprung up like dandelions in the summertime. The passage of time has all but eliminated the tobacco industry and the textile mills, but the region has adapted and now is home to technology companies and entrepreneurs. Much of this is due to the large universities that dot the landscape of the Piedmont, such as the University of North Carolina, North Carolina State, Duke and Wake Forest. People from all around the world are attracted to these places, looking for great schools and safe neighborhoods. Most find what they are looking for, but for some, this is a place where their dreams turned to a nightmare.

The Lucky Strike smokestack and water tower in Durham, North Carolina, are monuments of times gone by in the Piedmont region of central North Carolina when tobacco was king. *Author's collection.*

Chapter 9
POOR ELLEN SMITH

Ellen Smith was a pretty girl. She was seventeen years old in 1892 and was working at the beautiful new Hotel Zinzendorf in Winston-Salem, North Carolina. She was a girl who could catch the eye of any nice young boy she desired, but like so many nice pretty young ladies in the history of sad stories, she found herself desperately in love with a bad boy. It is believed that Ellen Smith was born in 1874 because of a listing in the 1880 census of a six-year-old mulatto girl in Yadkin County, mulatto being a catchall term of the time for anyone of mixed race. It is not known if Ellen was mixed with African American or Native American heritage. Being "mulatto" in 1892, Ellen had done well by finding work in such a swanky place as the Hotel Zinzendorf. The hotel was the crown jewel of Winston-Salem at the time, but it was there that she came into the orbit of a wild young man named Peter DeGraff.

DeGraff was in his early twenties in 1892 when he met Ellen. He was already known around Winston-Salem as a playboy and a cad. He was a drinker and a gambler and was fast with the ladies. He had several run-ins with the law, including an arrest for carrying a gun. He had escaped jail and fled to Virginia until he felt it was safe to come home. That summer of 1892, he was also working at the Hotel Zinzendorf and had started an affair with Ellen, who was smitten with the scoundrel, against all advice from the people she worked with, who told her she was playing with fire and was on the way to a broken heart at the very least. She refused to see past the veneer of Peter DeGraff.

The Hotel Zinzendorf, where Ellen Smith met Peter DeGraff. *Courtesy of the Forsyth County Public Library Photograph Collection.*

They met regularly in the nearby woods outside the hotel and spent many hours doing things that young lovers do. The long summer days and hot summer nights in North Carolina were the perfect setting for the romance that was developing. Things changed though when Ellen became pregnant. Peter was a wild horse who would not be tamed. His first instinct at the prospect of being chained down was to run. He had a note delivered to Ellen by a friend telling her that he was done. He wanted to end the relationship and be done with her before he had to be tied down in any way. She was devastated, to say the least. Ellen locked herself in her room and cried for days, inconsolable to any attempt to soothe her pain. The talk of the breakup increased because of her absence from the hotel, and Peter found himself feeling chained down by the constant looks and whispers of townsfolk. As long as Ellen was alive, he would be on the spot and expected to take care of her. Everyone was looking to him to do the right thing and settle down. On July 20, 1892, he sent her another note stating that he wanted to meet her in "their spot" in the woods by the hotel to reconcile.

"Their spot," she thought as she read his note. Closing her eyes and holding the note close to her chest, she let the happy times rush back to her,

Ellen Smith was murdered by her lover, Peter DeGraff. *Courtesy of* Winston-Salem Sentinel.

and she smiled in her room for the first time in days. She cleaned herself up, put on a nice dress and briskly walked down the street to the woods to wait for her lover to arrive. That afternoon, as people saw her emerge from her room and walk by them smiling, few would have thought they were seeing Ellen Smith alive for the last time.

On the morning of July 21, guests of the hotel came to the front desk and said that an unknown man had told them there was a body in the woods behind the hotel and had then disappeared as quickly as he had appeared. This happened a few times that morning and convinced the hotel manager that he needed go and check it out. There in the woods they found the body of Ellen Smith, shot through the heart one single time. She had powder burns on her dress from the gunshot, which had obviously been done at very close range. She had not been running; she had been with someone she trusted. Her trust had been what ultimately killed her. As the residents of Winston came out of their homes to the woods, they began to form into a posse. There was only one suspect— Peter DeGraff—and they were going to find him.

The sheriff of Forsyth County issued an arrest warrant for DeGraff, but he was nowhere to be found. The crowd searched through his parents' house and all the haunts that he was known to hit but with no luck. Time went by, and people lost interest. When DeGraff emerged from his hiding spot, the sheriff had lost interest in doing anything about him, and he resumed his life hiding in plain sight on the streets of Winston-Salem. It was not until a new sheriff, Sheriff McArthur, was elected that Peter was taken into custody and charged with the murder of Ellen Smith. When he was arrested, he was found in the woods behind the Hotel Zinzendorf at the scene of Ellen's murder—a fact that would not serve him well in his pursuit of saving his own life during his trial.

The trial was held in the summer of 1883. Peter DeGraff pleaded not guilty of the murder of Ellen Smith. The trial was front-page news due to the nature of the murder and the steamy details of the affair that came out daily. People were dying

Peter DeGraff sang "Am I Not a Soldier of the Cross?" as he climbed the gallows to be hanged. *Courtesy of* Winston-Salem Sentinel.

to hear the latest gossip every day when the paper came out. DeGraff maintained his innocence throughout the trial but sealed his fate when he said that he had read a book that said if a killer returned to the scene of the crime and said some magic words, then the deceased would come back and what had been done would be undone. The prosecution was quick to point out that he was arrested in the woods where the murder had taken place. The jury deliberated for twelve hours and came back with a guilty verdict. DeGraff appealed several times, but the judgment stood: he was sentenced to hang.

On February 8, 1894, in front of a crowd estimated to be in the range of six thousand people from all over the state, Peter DeGraff, Bible in hand, climbed the steps of the gallows in Forsyth County. As he climbed, he sang, "Am I a Soldier of the Cross?"

> *Am I a soldier of the Cross*
> *A follower of the Lamb*
> *And shall I fear to own His cause*
> *Or blush to speak His name*

When he reached the top, a noose was put around his neck, and he handed the Bible to his brother Lee, who was standing by his side. He asked to make a statement, and the crowd quieted. He said that he had loved Ellen and had wanted to marry her. He gave no justification for killing her but confessed and said he had been drunk at the time. When he finished, the executioner pulled the hood down over his head and pulled the lever. Peter DeGraff swung from the rope, paying the price for taking the lives of Ellen and her unborn child. It would be the last public execution in Forsyth County. His body was taken to the potter's field and buried anonymously.

Chapter 10
NAOMI WISE

The story of Naomi Wise and her murder is unique because of its age and longevity in the history of North Carolina. Having been killed in 1807, her story dates back the furthest of all the occurrences in this book. With so much time having passed and so few official records having existed or surviving until today, it is hard to know what really happened. Much of her story is told through poems and songs from long ago. Backwoods storytellers and folk singers have carried this tragedy through generations and made it possible for young Naomi to live on today in the consciousness of those who hear her story.

The story of Naomi Wise begins in Randolph County, North Carolina, in the year 1807. William and Mary Adams had taken in a young orphan girl named Naomi as an indentured servant. She worked on their farm and in the house cooking, cleaning and tending animals. As she grew, she became a very lovely young lady. Although she was a servant, William and Mary considered her their daughter, and the love they expressed was returned by Naomi, who considered them her family. As she went about her chores for the Adamses, she began to notice a tall stranger riding by their farm on Saturday evenings. The stranger was the tall, dark and handsome type, well built and sturdy looking. Naomi tried her best to look without staring as he rode by, but he began to notice her attention.

His name was Jonathan Lewis, a resident of Guilford County, but he was employed by Benjamin Elliot in Asheboro as a clerk in his store. He boarded with Elliot during the week while he worked and on Saturdays would make

The murder of Naomi Wise by Jonathan Lewis. *Illustration by Anna Grace Hand.*

the long ride back to his family's farm, passing by the Adams place every week. He began to notice Naomi just as she had been noticing him, playing the same game of taking a peek when he thought she was not looking but always admiring her from a distance. He began to notice that when he glanced at her, she was stealing glances at him.

One day as Jonathan was riding by, he noticed Naomi was getting water from the well. He saw his chance and rode over to her. He introduced himself and, with a smile and a twinkle in his eye, asked for a drink. Gladly, she fetched him a ladle, and they began to talk. Jonathan even got off his horse and helped her take the water bucket back up to the house and met the Adamses. From that point on, Jonathan would not fail to stop and see her every week. They began to fall more and more in love each time they were together. Naomi began to think about marriage and was making plans in anticipation of what she felt was a proposal coming very soon.

Unfortunately for Naomi, Jonathan's mother had other plans. She was determined for Jonathan to marry a girl of stature, and that was certainly not Naomi. His mother was intent on his getting married to Mr. Elliot's daughter Hattie so that he could take over the store one day. His mother insisted, and Jonathan began to court Hattie, all the while stopping every Saturday to be with Naomi. Eventually, there came a time of choosing for Jonathan. He asked Hattie to be his bride and began to pass the Adams farm without stopping. Naomi watched him ride by in the distance, careful not to look over at her. She stood and watched helplessly as her heart died a little each time.

Soon the rumor mill churned up the news to Naomi about the engagement of Jonathan Lewis to Hattie Elliot. She couldn't believe what she was hearing and ran out to confront him the next Saturday evening. She found a much different man than the one she thought she had known. He was aloof and mean to her. He told her that he had no idea she harbored these feelings for him and that he did not reciprocate them. He said he had never loved her to begin with and there had never been a future between them. As he turned to ride away, Naomi had one last thing to tell him that stopped him in his tracks.

Naomi came home that night and finished her chores. Mrs. Adams had been worried about her since Jonathan had stopped coming around. She had really liked the young man and knew that Naomi was dealing with a broken heart. She had noticed her go after Jonathan that night and saw them talking. In her mind, Mrs. Adams was done with him anyway because he had hurt Naomi so, but she knew Naomi loved him and held out hope. Mrs. Adams watched her come back and finish her work in the yard. She asked her if everything was all right when she came into the house, but Naomi just said "fine" and went to bed. Naomi looked better, but she kept the resolution to herself and wouldn't share what was said with Mrs. Adams over the next few days.

One morning in early April, Naomi grabbed the buckets and told the Adamses she was going to the well to bring back water. It was the last time they were to see her alive. When she didn't come back, a search party was raised, and they set off looking for her. By nightfall, they had found a set of footprints in the mud by the river that led to a stump. Going away from the stump were hoof prints. It was obvious that she had used the stump to mount a horse and ride off. The tracks were followed as far as they could, but eventually the trail was lost. It was not long though before the body of Naomi Wise was found washed ashore downstream on the Deep River. She had been strangled to death and thrown into the river. When the body was examined, it was discovered that Naomi had been with child at the time of her death.

Everybody knew who had killed the poor girl. Jonathan had found out she was carrying his child the night she had met him on his ride home, and he had vowed to take her away and marry her. She met him at the stump and rode off with him with the thought of being whisked away by her true love who was going to take care of her and her child. Jonathan rode to a ford on the Deep River and dismounted, helping her down as well. When she was down, he fell upon her and choked the life out of her right there on the bank of the river. When he felt the life go out of her, he pushed her body into the water and watched it float downstream. Thinking the brown water had carried his trouble away, he remounted his horse and rode away.

He was quickly caught and thrown into jail. Charged with Naomi's murder, he sat in jail waiting for his trail, which was scheduled to take place on October 6 of that year. Jonathan had no intention of waiting to see how the jury would find him, and he escaped on October 9. He was caught again two years later, but he was only charged the second time for escaping from jail. He was found guilty, paid a fine and spent thirty more days in jail. Somehow, he was never tried for the crime of killing Naomi Wise. Her young life was never avenged and justice was never served for her. Were it not for her story being passed down through the generations, she would be just a forgotten girl who found that a mistake she made led to her death. Among other tributes, Doc Watson and Bob Dylan have recorded the folk song "Naomi Wise." Millions of people have heard this song not knowing that there once was a lovestruck young girl who died at the hands of the one person she wanted to be with above all others.

Chapter 11
ALL-AMERICAN KILLER

The crowd of turquoise, black and silver erupted and sprang to their feet. Voices strained and hands went up in the air, signaling a touchdown. Pandemonium! Rae Carruth dropped the ball to the ground by his side and ran along the backside of the end zone, strutting for the crowd. The adulation was intoxicating, and he could stay in that moment forever. Every eye in Bank of America Stadium was watching him with adoration and excitement. He had made it, and nothing was going to take this from him. Nothing.

Carruth was born in Sacramento, California, and had spent his whole childhood there. Early on, he was singled out on the football field as a star. So much so that when it came time for college, he was able to attend the University of Colorado at Boulder on an athletic scholarship. Carruth also excelled in the NCAA and was drafted twenty-seventh overall in the first round of the 1996 NFL draft by the Carolina Panthers, who play in Charlotte, North Carolina. His stock was on the rise in the NFL. During his rookie season, he was voted to the All-Rookie team. Everything was going his way until he broke his foot in the first game of the 1997 season and found himself watching from the sidelines for the rest of the year while he healed. His star was still shining, but he got a glimpse of what he could lose if he wasn't on the field.

Off the field, he was having a different kind of struggle. He had gotten his girlfriend in college pregnant and had shown little interest in the son she bore him. In 1996, she had taken him to court to force him to pay child support. Grudgingly, he complied with the court order, but he resented sending his money to her. Since living in Charlotte, he had begun dating a young woman named Cherica Adams, who was a Charlotte native and was working on a real estate career. Cherica found her relationship with Carruth to be very complicated. Sometimes he was in love and wanted to spend time with her, and sometimes he could be very cold and mean. They were on again, off again for a while, but during the period when he was recovering from his injuries, he renewed his relationship with Cherica. The time they spent together was special to her, and during this time, she became pregnant. When Rae found out, he turned cold once more to Cherica, and her heart was broken. He did not want to have a repeat of his previous situation and did not want to have to write another check every month for a child he did not want.

On the night of November 16, 1999, Carruth asked Cherica to go to a movie. She was excited and had hopes that he was changing his mind about their situation. She was eight months pregnant and had been having her doubts that Rae Carruth was going to have any active role in her baby's life. They had a great night, and after the movie, Carruth asked if he could spend the night at her apartment. She agreed happily, and he told her to take him by his house to get his car and then follow him in her car to her apartment. As they drove along Rea Road in Charlotte, he slowed down to a stop in the middle of the road. Confused, Cherica noticed that the car behind her had pulled up beside her. As she looked over at the car, she was horrified to see a man pointing a gun at her. Five shots rang out and broke the silence of the night around them. The shots penetrated the car, hitting her four times. She looked up and could see Rae's eyes in the rearview mirror coldly watching her. She was devastated as she saw both cars drive away. Alone, she began to drive slowly down Rea Road and called 911 on her cellphone.

She drove into a neighborhood and onto someone's lawn, blowing her horn to try to draw attention. Desperate for help, she stayed on the phone with the 911 emergency operators, speaking through her pain and trying to tell them everything she could about her surroundings so they could find her. She told them what had happened and made sure they knew that she had been following her baby's daddy, "Rae Carruth, number 89." They finally found her and took her to the hospital, where the baby was delivered by C section while doctors also worked to save her life. Once the baby was safe, they went to work on Cherica, desperately trying to save her life. She remained in critical condition, but bravely, she asked the nurse for a pen and paper to write down as much information as she could for the police. Finally, she slipped into a coma after hours of struggling to stay alert to ensure the authorities had all the information she could provide.

At the hospital that night, Rae Carruth showed up and sat on the floor in the waiting room. He never asked about Cherica or the baby; he just sat there, almost as if he was just there to make an appearance. Cherica's mother confronted him about the shooting, but he denied that he knew anything. Over the course of the next few days, police attempted to question him, but he was unwilling to work with them. They began to dig into his phone records and bank records. This led them to two men who had very shady pasts: Michael Kennedy and Van Brett Watkins. The police found Watkins first, and he was more than willing to talk, telling the police a fantastic story about the time leading up to the murder and even admitting to being the triggerman for the murder himself.

Watkins claimed that he had been doing odd jobs for Rae Carruth, who, after finding out he was an ex-con, approached him with a proposition. Carruth said he would pay him $3,000 to beat up Cherica and force her to have a miscarriage. Watkins told him he was willing but asked for a deposit to see if he was serious. Carruth immediately left the house, went to an ATM and withdrew $500 cash. He brought it back and made it clear he was very serious. Later, police corroborated that Carruth had made these withdrawals exactly when Watkins claimed he did.

Watkins claimed that as the weeks went by, he was contacted by Carruth several times asking when he was going to do it and even making suggestions as to how he could do it. Soon, Carruth's plans turned from killing her child to killing them both. He upped the ante with an offer of $6,000 when the job was done. Watkins told police that he began to have second thoughts, but Carruth would not let up. Watkins wanted to back out but claims Carruth let him know that just like he had hired him to take care of Cherica, he could hire someone to take care of Watkins as well if he backed out. Watkins claimed that he was forced to act to save himself.

The night the murders were to take place was determined, and the plan was put into place. Rae Carruth called Cherica Adams and asked her to a movie. She came to his house, and he drove her out for the date. When they finished the movie, Carruth made the call to Watkins and the other accomplices. After the movie, as planned, he told her he wanted to spend the night at her apartment. Watkins and Kennedy waited at Rae

NFL star Rae Carruth orchestrated the death of his girlfriend after he found out she was pregnant. *Illustration by Anna Grace Hand.*

Carruth's house for Cherica to bring him by for his car and then began to follow them. Rae was in front of her, and they followed closely behind, with Kennedy driving and Watkins in the passenger seat. Just as they planned, Rae waited until they got to a secluded location and stopped the car in the road. This was their signal, and they pulled up alongside her. Watkins fired five shots into her car, and they drove off. Based on this information and the other evidence, Carruth was arrested, let out on bail and told not to leave town.

After fighting for her life in a coma, Cherica passed away, and Carruth's bail was immediately revoked. He was charged with murder, and a warrant was issued for his arrest. The Charlotte-Mecklenburg Police Department began the search for him, but he was nowhere to be found. They followed every lead they could get, and by the next night, he was found hiding in the trunk of a car at a motel in Tennessee. They brought him back, and he was put on trial for the murder of Cherica Adams. At the trial, the star witness was Cherica Adams herself. Her bravery in making the 911 call and telling the police as much information as she could was helpful to the prosecution. Also, her handwritten notes in the moments before she slipped into a coma were damning to the defense. Van Brett Watkins was a belligerent and hostile witness who proved that he was a ruthless killer by the way he carried himself in the courtroom. He had taken a plea bargain and spoke freely about his involvement. He bantered openly with the defense attorney. At the end of the trial, the jury did not have to fight over the matter of Rae Carruth's guilt. Their problem was with the plea deal that Watkins had received. They felt that it was not right to give Rae Carruth a stiffer penalty for planning the murders than the actual killer. In the end, they convicted him of second-degree murder and conspiracy. He was given twenty-three years in prison.

Out of darkness often comes light. Chancellor Adams, who bears a striking resemblance to his father, now lives with his grandmother. She took him on and has allowed her love of Cherica to flow to him. He has brain damage from the shooting and has many challenges today, but his life represents the bravery and the fighting spirit of his mom. Cherica was determined to bring him into this world even as she was slipping out of it. Rae Carruth was released from prison in October 2018 and has moved away from North Carolina and changed his name.

Chapter 12
MICHAEL PETERSON

Early on the morning of December 9, 2001, the Durham Emergency Service received a call from a distraught man who said his wife had fallen down the stairs and was bleeding badly. When first responders got to the lush mansion in the Forest Hills neighborhood, they found a woman lying in a pool of blood at the bottom of a back staircase. They knew they were too late because of the amount of blood and the blank stare on the woman's face. Her husband, visibly upset, paced and told the officers and paramedics that they had spent the night at home and watched a video. They had drunk a lot, he said, and his wife was drunk. After sitting out back by the pool talking until early in the morning, they had decided to go to bed. She had gone inside, and he stayed back for a while to turn off all the lights and lock up. He told them that when he came in about 2:40 a.m., he found her there at the bottom of the stairs.

The police became immediately suspicious of the man. While they were working on his wife trying to resuscitate her, he went to his study and got on his computer. They found it odd that with his wife having just passed away, he would go straight to the computer. Officers noticed that blood was spattered high up on the wall above where it could be expected from just a fall, and the amount of blood was excessive. In the kitchen, there was a bottle of champagne and two glasses by the sink. One glass had fingerprints, but the other glass did not. The sink smelled of alcohol, as if the champagne had been poured down the drain recently. Responding officers called in Durham homicide investigator Art Holland to investigate the scene. When he got there and began to interview the man, he knew exactly who he was speaking with. Or at least he thought he did; there was another side to this man—a side that very few people knew about.

Michael Peterson was born in Nashville, Tennessee, and had first come to Durham to attend Duke University. At Duke, he was the editor of the student paper and the head of his fraternity. After completing his undergraduate degree, he attended classes at the University of North Carolina in Chapel Hill at the law school. He got a job with the Department of Defense and moved to Germany, where he met his first wife, Patricia. In 1968, he enlisted in the United States Marine Corps and was soon sent to Vietnam. He was in the marines until 1971, when he was medically discharged due to a traffic accident that left him with a permanent limp. At the conclusion of his time in the marines, he was awarded the Bronze Star and the Silver Star for valor during his time in Vietnam.

After his military service was over, Peterson and his wife continued to live in Germany, where they became friends with George and Elizabeth Ratliff. George passed away a few years later, leaving Elizabeth alone with her two daughters. The Petersons helped out as much as they could and became very close to Elizabeth—so close that when Elizabeth also unexpectedly died, Michael Peterson became the guardian of her two daughters and took them in as his own. In 1987, the Petersons divorced, and Michael moved back to Durham with his two children and the Ratliff girls. He became a novelist and a writer for the *Durham Herald Sun*, where he was critical of the Durham Police Department and the district attorney. He even unsuccessfully ran for mayor. He settled back into the community that he had adopted many years before as a college student, but this time he was someone of stature.

In 1989, he met an attractive executive from Northern Telecomm (Nortel) in the Research Triangle Park named Kathleen Atwater. Kathleen was bright and very social. She had also graduated from Duke University and had, in fact, been the first female student in the school's engineering department. She had a great business career and had moved rapidly up the ranks in a world dominated by men. They fell in love and moved in together that same year. They quickly became a power couple in the social circles of Durham and by 1997 had decided to get married and combine their families. They moved into the largest home in the community of Forest Hills. What seemed like the happy ending that anyone would dream of was the beginning of a nightmare. The home that Kathleen loved to entertain in would in just a few short years be the site of her untimely death.

Michael Peterson maintained his story to the police that Kathleen was intoxicated with Valium and wine and that he had found her at the bottom of the back stairs after turning off the lights at the pool. When the toxicology report came back, the police learned that her blood alcohol level was 0.07, below the standards of intoxication. Also, the injuries she sustained and blood spatters were not consistent with an accidental fall. She had sustained severe injuries on her head and neck, including seven lacerations that were consistent with blunt force strikes. The medical examiner also determined that she died of blood loss ninety minutes to two hours after the injuries had occurred, which would have been impossible if Michael Peterson's timeline were correct. Shortly after her death, he was arrested and charged with murder. He hired a team of high-priced attorneys and pleaded not guilty.

The trial soon became a circus and the talk of the state and nation. The defense brought in Dr. Henry Lee, the forensic expert who had gained fame in the O.J. Simpson trial. He disputed the district attorney's claim that the blood splatters were not consistent with a fall, even standing and spitting ketchup against a white board during the trial to illustrate to the jury how the blood could have ended up on the wall in the manner that it did. Even with an all-star defense team, Michael Peterson's secrets began to spill out as the jury, and everyone else, learned of his secret bisexual lifestyle and how he had paid male prostitutes for sex. Peterson claimed that Kathleen knew of this part of his life and was accepting. Then there were the money problems. Although Kathleen made a great salary at Nortel, she was in fear of being laid off, while Michael had not published a book in some time. The home they lived in was very expensive; even just the upkeep was astronomical at times. Kathleen had a $1.5 million life insurance policy, of which Michael was the beneficiary, and the prosecutors used this as his motive, portraying him as a man who was unwilling to lose his stature or his lifestyle for anything.

There were two huge bombshells during the trial. The first was the revelation that in 1985, Elizabeth Ratliff, whose death led to Michael Peterson becoming the guardian of her two girls, had been found dead at the bottom of the stairs at her apartment complex. Her death being so similar to Kathleen's motivated the prosecution to have her body exhumed and an autopsy performed. The autopsy showed similar head injuries to those suffered by Kathleen, and the cause of death was changed from accidental death to homicide. The second bombshell was on the part of the defense. The prosecution had insisted from the beginning that the murder weapon was a custom-made blow poke that had been a gift from Kathleen's sister years before. It fit the description of the size and shape of what the medical examiner described had caused the lacerations. The blow poke had been known to be in the house but was nowhere to be found by investigators after the murder. At the end of the trial, the defense presented for evidence the missing blow poke, covered in dust, retrieved from the garage under some boxes. The amount of dust on the blow poke eliminated it as a potential murder weapon, and the defense had what was for a small moment a victory.

It wouldn't last long. When the jury brought back the verdict on October 10, 2003, they judged him guilty of first-degree murder. Michael Peterson was taken into custody and taken to his new home at the Nash Correctional Center near Rocky Mount, North Carolina. But his story was not over yet, as Peterson had a lucky break coming his way. The North Carolina State Bureau of Investigations came under fire for flawed investigative tactics. One of the primary witnesses against Peterson was demoted and fired from the SBI, prompting the state's attorney general, Roy Cooper, to allow Michael Peterson to receive a retrial. In December 2011, he was released on bond, and after being unable to find sufficient evidence to show his innocence, and after not being able to have the trial thrown out, Michael Peterson pleaded guilty to voluntary manslaughter. It was what is known as an Alford Plea, which means that he was not admitting guilt but that the state had enough evidence to convict him of murder yet again. The judge sentenced him to no more than eighty-six months in prison and took into account the time that he had already served, which exceeded this time. Michael Peterson was, and remains to this day, a free man once more.

Chapter 13

HENRY WALLACE

Henry Wallace was born in Barnwell, South Carolina, and lived what most would say was a very inconsequential life. He was the son of a single mother who worked long hours and did her best to raise her son and daughter. Neighbors and family members would remember him as a normal child. He was on the cheerleading squad and the student council while in high school. After graduating, he tried several colleges and worked as a disc jockey for a local station before joining the Navy Reserve in 1985. He was fired from his DJ job for stealing CDs and later was arrested for breaking and entering. When the navy learned of these charges, he was given an honorable discharge. In 1987, he married, but the marriage soon fell apart. After his discharge from the navy and his marriage ending, he worked at several fast-food restaurants before becoming a supervisor at Taco Bell in East Charlotte, North Carolina. He seemed to people who knew him to have finally found a place that he would stay at for more than a few months, but under the surface, he had a secret life. No one would have guessed that this man was responsible for a reign of terror that led to the deaths of eleven young women.

Wallace first killed before he had left Barnwell for Charlotte. He was twenty-four years old and recently discharged from the navy when he noticed a bright-eyed high school senior named Toshonda Bethea. He would give her rides home from school sometimes and make advances, but she always turned him down. One day, he took her to a wooded area instead of taking her home and demanded sex from her. When she refused yet again, he pulled a pistol on her and told her that she was going to do exactly what he wanted her to. After he was done assaulting her, he asked her if she planned on telling anyone. She said yes but then immediately said she would not. Wallace believed she would tell, and he attempted to strangle her, hoping to silence her. He drove to a pond about six miles outside Barnwell to dump her body, but when he got there, he discovered she was not dead. He strangled her again and cut her throat and wrists with a box cutter before putting her in the pond.

When she was found two weeks later, the coroner discovered that she had still been alive when she was put into the pond because of water in her lungs. Wallace was a suspect and was questioned by the local police about the murder. His car was searched for any blood or hair that belonged to Toshonda, but the police could find nothing. Without evidence, the police had to let him go. Wallace was not cooperative at all with the police and would not give them anything they could use against him. In 1992, he moved with his mother to Charlotte. He was able to find work easily in the fast-food industry and was soon a supervisor at Taco Bell.

Wallace's first murder in Charlotte took place in May 1992 when he picked up Sharon Nance. She was a convicted drug dealer and prostitute who was known by the police in East Charlotte. After she and Wallace had sex, she demanded payment from him, and he beat her to death in his car. Wallace drove her to a spot along the railroad tracks and dumped her body there. She was found a few days later, but the police never questioned Wallace about the murder. Just a few months later, he entered the apartment of his girlfriend with a key. She was not home, but her roommate, Caroline Love, was. Wallace tried to have sex with her, but she rebuked him. He raped her and strangled her to death with the cord from a curling iron. He took her body and dumped it in a wooded area. When his girlfriend got concerned about her missing roommate, Wallace even drove to the police station to file a missing person's report with her. So far, he was not on their radar at all.

Between February 1993 and February 1994, Wallace killed five more times. All of the women were either coworkers, friends of coworkers or friends of friends. They were all young black women. Wallace raped and strangled them and dumped their bodies around East Charlotte. These women were Shawna Hawk, Audrey Spain, Valencia Jumper, Michelle Stinson and Vanessa Mack. During this time, the police never questioned him about any of these murders. He was able to stalk his prey unmolested by the police, who did not even know yet what they were dealing with. In February 1994, he was arrested for shoplifting, but the police did not have any evidence of any other crimes he had committed, so he was back on the street in a matter of hours—and back on the hunt for victims.

The climax of his killing spree came in March 1994 after a series of brutal murders and finally a mistake on the part of Wallace, which led to a break in the case. On March 8, he broke into the house of Betty Jean Baucom, who was friends with his girlfriend, and raped and robbed her. He stole items from her house and even stole her car. He sold the stolen items to a pawnshop and left the abandoned car in a shopping center parking lot. That night, he returned to the same apartment complex and raped Brandi Henderson, a neighbor of Betty Jean, while she held her baby son in her arms. Wallace strangled the baby too, but luckily, the boy survived. When the bodies were found in the same apartment complex, the police stepped up patrols in East Charlotte. Despite the increased police presence, Wallace strangled and stabbed Debra Ann Slaughter, whose body was found just a few days later in the area.

Wallace was brazen and began to feel like he would never be stopped, but stealing the car and abandoning it had been the mistake that police were waiting for him to make. Charlotte-Mecklenburg Police Department detectives searched the car, and a handprint was lifted off the driver's side window. It belonged to Henry Wallace, who was arrested and, upon questioning, began a marathon of confessions for the murder of Betty Jean Baucom as well as the other ten women he had raped and killed.

The community reacted harshly to the Charlotte-Mecklenburg Police Department. Many in the community, including the families of the victims, claimed that if the victims had blond hair and blue eyes, the police would have not only noticed the connection to the murders sooner but also would have expended more effort to solve the crimes. The CMPD chief spoke out and said that the presence of a serial killer was not known until the three bodies were found in the course of four days. The other murders, they said, lacked witnesses and all had variances that led them to believe they were not related. Still, the fact that all of the victims were black and working class strained relations between the residents and the police in the community of East Charlotte.

Henry Wallace's trial was delayed with arguments over DNA evidence and venue change requests. The defense attorney argued that Wallace was suffering from mental illness, but the jury was not convinced and convicted him of nine counts of first-degree murder and sentenced him to death. Wallace sits today on death row at Central Prison in Raleigh waiting for his fate. The hunter now sits in a cage awaiting death. Although he was given the chance that his victims never had, which was to defend himself, he will find that in the end his fate is the same as his victims'. His death might come slowly, looking through bars over many years, but it will come. Maybe then the families will feel some sense of justice for their loss.

Chapter 14

COACH STAGER LEFT A MESSAGE

Coach Russell Stager was gone, and that was a sad fact that his students had been dealing with. He was the baseball coach and driver's education teacher at Durham High School and was loved by all. He had died suddenly a few months before when his wife accidentally shot him in bed while trying to remove a loaded pistol from underneath his pillow. His absence was still something that the students and faculty were trying to get used to. In the coaches' office, a student was cleaning out a locker when he found a cassette tape. He put it into a tape player, and the voice was unmistakable; the words chilling. It was Coach Stager, and he was talking about how he feared for his life. Three days before his death, Coach Stager had chronicled his concerns just in case his worst fears came true. They had.

On the morning of February 1, 1988, Deputy Paul Hornebuckle received a call from dispatch to respond to an accidental shooting. When he arrived at the house, he spoke to a visually upset Barbara Stager, Russell's wife, who said she had accidentally shot him in the back of the head. She said that Russ had been keeping a loaded .25-caliber pistol under his pillow lately because of crime in the neighborhood. Early in the morning, she heard her son wake up and go to the bathroom, she explained. She became frightened that Russ was going to hear him, wake up and shoot him before he realized it was not an intruder. She reached under his pillow to get the pistol, and as she pulled it out, it went off in her hand. The deputy took the report and spoke to the first responders who had arrived on the scene before him. They had been dispatched from the volunteer fire department in the area, and many of them knew Russ and Barbara. They all told the deputy that they were good Christian people, real pillar-of-the-community types.

Russell Stager was a born-and-raised native to Durham, North Carolina, where he graduated from Durham High School and married his high school sweetheart, Jo Lynn Snow. Their marriage did not last long, but they were able to part as friends. Russ went to work at his alma mater as the baseball coach and driver's education teacher; his students loved him. Coach Stager was a guy everyone liked to be around, yet his life seemed to be falling apart by the time he was forty years old. He had remarried Barbara Ford, a widow with two young sons. Her first husband had shot himself while cleaning his gun, and she was raising the boys on her own. Everything was great at first but began to fall apart. Constant money problems from Barbara's excessive spending, hints of infidelity and then certainty of her cheating strained the marriage every day. These were facts that most people did not know due to the careful act that they played around friends, family and their church congregation.

The shooting was initially ruled an accidental shooting, just like Barbara had said it was, but then the sheriff's department received an unexpected

Durham High School, where Russell Stager coached baseball and left an audiotape expressing his concern for his life. *Author's collection.*

letter from an unexpected source. Russ's ex-wife, Jo Lynn, sent a letter to the investigators telling them that she had been in contact with Russell for the past several months and he had been confiding in her that Barbara was not the good Christian woman she made herself out to be. He had told her that she had been kiting checks and accumulating debt at a staggering rate. She had forged his signature on many bad checks and was always staying one step ahead of creditors. She had an appetite for expensive things and always wanted new cars and boats and had even bought them matching Rolex watches. That was not all. She also had an appetite for other men. Russ had caught her at least once in the act of adultery, and he was sure there had been more. He had eerily told Jo Lynn to look into it if anything ever happened to him.

Sergeant Richard Buchanan took over the case as the lead investigator, and along with the information from Jo Lynn, he began to look into the Stagers' relationship under the surface. He found that not only was she right about the finances, but also Russ had been insured for a large amount of money shortly before he died, with Barbara as the sole beneficiary. All of these things gave Buchanan a motive to work with, but there was also the "accident" that led to Russ's death. Russ was in the National Guard and had a lot of weapons training. It made no sense that a man who had that much experience with firearms would put a loaded gun under his pillow as he slept. Next there was the forensic evidence. The bullet entered into his head at a downward angle, and the tests for the pistol showed that the shell casing would eject back and to the right every time. At the scene, the shell casing was found right behind Russ's body on the bed when it should have been at the foot of the bed. If the shooting happened like Barbara said it did, the bullet should have entered into his head at an upward angle. Also, she claimed the weapon had a hair trigger, but testing showed that it took a substantial amount of force to discharge it. The trigger had to have been pulled intentionally.

Sergeant Buchanan found out through his investigation from Jo Lynn's tip that Barbara's first husband, Larry Ford, had also died. He had been shot accidentally in the chest while cleaning his .25-caliber pistol. Ford's family had wanted an autopsy and investigation, but Barbara had insisted he be buried as soon as possible, and the case was closed. Accidental shooting? It was all adding up against her, and Buchanan was ready to pounce. Barbara Stager was arrested for the murder of Russ Stager, much to the confusion and surprise of those who had thought they knew her. They had no idea of the dark side that she hid.

While she was awaiting trial with the evidence that Buchanan had compiled, a student was cleaning out a locker at Durham High School when he came across the tape. When he played it, the voice was unmistakable. It was Coach Stager. Coach was talking about his wife on the tapes, describing how she had woken him up in the middle of the night the last few nights and tried to give him what she said were aspirin to help him sleep. He wondered out loud on the recording why she would wake him up and tell him she was worried about his sleep. He was becoming afraid for his life and questioned the circumstances surrounding her first husband's death. Chillingly, the tape was made just three days before he was murdered. The tape was a bombshell for the prosecution.

The authorities used this audiotape along with the other evidence to secure the conviction of Barbara Stager. It is a rare occurrence in criminal law when a murder victim can testify on his or her own behalf. The eerie sound of Russell Stager's voice from beyond the grave talking about his concern for his life and his suspicions about his wife was enough to nail the coffin shut on any hopes that Barbara had of being a free woman again. She was convicted of murder, but later her sentence was reduced to life in prison. She has been eligible for parole before but each time has been denied, much to the credit of Jo Lynn, who has remained loyal to her commitment to see justice done for Russell. She was an integral part of putting his killer away, and she has been a constant opponent of Barbara Stager's freedom ever since.

Chapter 15

BROTHER AGAINST BROTHER

Kristine Ray pulled up to the front of the store and drove over the parcel pickup bell like she had done many times before. John Ray, her husband, was the grocery manager at the Food Lion grocery store on the corner of Six Forks and Strickland Roads in Raleigh and often found himself closing the store. He had called her around 10:40 p.m. and said it should be a pretty early night for them and she could go ahead and come to get him. The store closed at 11:00 p.m. every night, and she would usually drive over the bell and he would come out and let her know if he was done or would be a few more minutes. She sat waiting in her car for him to come out, but this night was different. She waited and waited, but he never came. Finally, she got out of the car and walked to the store's entrance. She knocked and looked inside but saw no one. Anxiety began to build in her stomach, and she felt that something was just not right. She got back in her car and drove around to the back of the store, where she knew there was a call button that truck drivers use to call inside the store when they arrive with their deliveries. When she still could not get a response, she drove to a payphone and called 911.

The Raleigh Police Department dispatched Officer Mike Liptak, who arrived around midnight. When he peered into the window, he saw no one inside as well. He walked across the front of the store to the other entrance and looked in. He could see from that vantage point that the safe door was open and there were tills on the floor in front of it. He returned to his car and called for backup. He then drove around the store to the back, where he found one of the doors was ajar. While other police units were responding to Liptak's call, the RPD called into the security system's central service operations and had the assistant manager of the store dispatched to accompany the officers into the store. When the backup officers arrived, they secured the store and entered the building.

Immediately upon opening the door, they saw a body lying on the concrete floor in the stockroom, shot in the back of the head. The officers spread out with guns drawn, not knowing what to expect. As they moved through the store, they found another body in the meat cooler. Blood was spreading across the clay-colored tiles —shot in the back of the head also. The assistant manager was able to identify the body in the stockroom as that of office assistant Mike Truelove and the body in the cooler as John Ray. The store became a crime scene, and they found that $2,300 was missing from the safe. Sometime between when the store had closed at eleven o'clock and when Kristine Ray drove over the parcel pickup bell, two young men had lost their lives.

The previous day, Ray McNeil had driven to South Carolina to pick up his friend Chris Thornhill and had brought him back to Raleigh on the eighteenth. Ray had been living with his brother Robert and had convinced Chris to come to Raleigh to get a place with him and look for work. Ray was a wayward young man who had spent time in the army but had been discharged for drinking and driving. He had worked various jobs, including briefly at Food Lion, where his brother Robert worked. On the way back from South Carolina, Thornhill showed Ray a .357 magnum that he had bought before he left. They got to Raleigh around 8:00 p.m. and checked into the Innkeeper Hotel. A few hours later, Ray left him at the hotel and took his gun. About midnight, Ray showed back up, looking dazed. He told Chris that he had met a guy and agreed to sell the gun to him at a gas station, but the man had stolen the gun and struck him in the ear with it. He told him he was having trouble hearing and his ear was in severe pain. Thornhill would later testify that when they had gotten to Raleigh and checked into the hotel, Ray McNeil had about $100, but by Monday when they left the Innkeeper, he had a vinyl bag with about $800 in it and a large roll of one-dollar bills with a rubber band around it.

The investigators at the crime scene already had a suspect in mind: Robert McNeil, Ray's brother. Robert had been a suspect in a previous robbery of the Food Lion where he worked at the Tower Shopping Center on New Bern Avenue in Raleigh. He had in fact been involved. He was the grocery manager at the time and had come to another store employee, Craig Stover, with a plan to rob the store and kill the assistant manager. Stover had balked at the idea of murder, but on the night of May 16, 1993, McNeil left the back door of the store unlocked as he and the assistant manager closed the store and finished up for the day. Stover, wearing a mask, came into the store and put a gun to McNeil's head. He stole $11,000 and locked the two men in a tractor-trailer that was parked at the store's loading dock and used for storage. Robert seemed too cool during the robbery and too comfortable with the situation. In the following days, he often laughed and joked about it with other associates and even with the assistant manager, who did not find the situation humorous at all. He was also spending money on large purchases that he would not usually be able to make.

Robert was questioned about the murders, and so was Ray because he was part of Robert's alibi; he said they had been together. The investigators traced the style of gun back to the gun that Chris Thornhill had bought in South Carolina and given to Ray, although they could not find the gun itself. They also found a palm print on the back door of the store that belonged to Ray McNeil. At the trial, the evidence was presented to the jury along with experts who testified on the acoustics of firing a gun in a meat cooler and the hearing loss and pain that it would cause. The brothers refused to testify against each other, but another brother, Michael, testified that Ray had confessed to the actual murders of the two men while saying that Robert had been in a dispute with the grocery manager, John Ray, and had orchestrated the robbery and murders. He also told the court that Ray had a very warped sense of loyalty and challenged his brother from the stand to defend himself if this was not true by testifying, but Ray remained silent. Michael's testimony, along with the other evidence, resulted in the death sentence for Ray McNeil, which was later reduced to life, and a life sentence for Robert McNeil.

There were four men in the store that night who know what happened. Only two are still able to tell the story, and they have maintained their silence for decades now. The loss of John Ray and Mike Truelove to their families, coworkers and communities was tragic. Like reading a book halfway through and ripping it in half, the rest of their stories will never be told. The Food Lion location closed soon afterward, and today the space is occupied by another chain store. People come and go in the store, and workers bring in stock and sort items in the backroom as they would if they worked at any other store. Most never know that where they stand is the site of such a grisly murder and the place where two lives were lost for a mere $2,300.

Chapter 16
CARTHAGE RAMPAGE

Carthage, North Carolina, the county seat of Moore County, is a tiny little town in the southern Piedmont. The little town is not known for its size and claims no celebrities and no great historic events. Before March 9, 2009, the town was mostly known for a legend that probably was not true anyway. It is said that when the Tyson Buggy Company shut down operations, Henry Ford offered to buy the plant to use for making his automobiles, but his offer was rejected. He moved on to open his plant in Detroit, Michigan, and the rest is history, or so they say. This story is more than likely not true because Ford was a native of Detroit anyway and probably never considered building his plant anywhere else. The people of Carthage would have been satisfied to go on forever being known for this urban legend or for nothing at all. That all changed on a clear March morning when a dark cloud descended on the town and the rage of an unstable man brought infamy to the little town in North Carolina.

Robert Stewart was born in Robeson County to working-class parents who soon moved to Moore County. Robert was a loner and was known to have a very volatile temper. He drifted through school, eventually dropping out in high school and doing odd jobs and painting work around town. He was married four times. His fourth marriage was a rekindling of his second marriage to Wanda Neal, who had divorced him for his abuse and temper years before. But Robert always felt that she was the one, and his third wife had to endure the continuous comparison between herself and Wanda. But

Robert Stewart entered the Pinelake Health and Rehabilitation Center with evil intentions on March 29, 2009. *Courtesy of William Jackson.*

Wanda, although she tried, could not change him, and in 2009, she decided that it was just not going to work for the second time. By February 2009, she had left him again, vowing that it was over for good this time. Robert had no intentions of letting her go again.

Shortly before 10:00 a.m. on March 9, Robert pulled into the parking lot of the Pinelake Rehabilitation Center, where Wanda worked, with a small arsenal and plans to show Wanda that he would decide when and how their marriage ended, not her. He stepped out of his vehicle and began to shoot into her parked car, shattering the windows and tearing holes in the seats. As he was shooting, a car pulled into the parking lot driven by Michael Cotton, who was coming to visit a relative. Robert squared up calmly, just like he was on the firing range, and shot into the car, hitting Michael in the shoulder. Cotton was able to drive to the building's entrance and run inside to sound the warning. Robert coolly left his rifle on the top of his car and took two pistols and a shotgun with him as he entered the building behind Cotton.

Inside, Coast Guard vet James Avant Jr. had heard the gunshots and met Michael Cotton at the door. He called out on the intercom for the staff to lock down the building. Wanda, who had been transferred just that morning to the more secured Alzheimer's wing of the facility, locked the room she was in and hid. Robert came though the entrance doors and began to stalk through the halls. Realizing Wanda was not in her usual work area, he headed for the Alzheimer's wing, stopping at rooms along the way and shooting residents. He even shot some residents as they sat in the hall in wheelchairs, unable to escape his wrath. Avant tried to engage Robert in an effort to stop him but was shot down in cold blood.

By this time, calls were coming in to the 911 dispatcher, who called it out to any law enforcement in the vicinity who could respond. Corporal Justin Garner was on duty and the closest to the facility that day. He arrived and entered the building without waiting for backup, hoping to stop the carnage and save as many people as he could. He followed the path of dead and injured people and came face to face with Robert, who had tried to enter the locked doors to the Alzheimer's unit to get to Wanda but had failed. Garner, pistol out and leveled on Robert, commanded that he drop his weapons. Robert just stared at him and did not comply. Again and again Garner ordered him to drop his weapons and put his hands up, but Robert was not done yet. He raised his shotgun to his waist, pointed in the officer's direction and fired, wounding him. Simultaneously, Garner fired, hitting Robert in the chest and taking him down. Garner limped over to him with his weapon pointed at him still, and he could see the defiance in Robert Stewart's eyes as he urged the officer on with the words "Kill me, kill me." Corporal Garner kicked the gun away from Robert and called out the need for medical assistance on the scene, exhibiting traits that a man like Robert Stewart could never understand: professionalism, courage and mercy.

Robert Stewart walked through the halls of the Pinelake Rehabilitation Center like the Angel of Death. *Illustration by Anna Grace Hand.*

Jerry Avant Jr.'s mother was a certified nursing assistant working there that day also. When she was told Jerry had been shot, she ran to him and held him in her arms as he bled. He asked her to pray with him, and they prayed until the ambulance came and took him away. That was the last time she saw him alive. Jerry died at the hospital shortly after going into surgery for his wounds. He died a hero trying to save others that day, along with seven others who were senselessly killed. The dead included residents Louise DeKler, Lillian Dunn, Tessie Garner, John Goldston, Bessie Hedrick, Margaret Johnson and

Jesse Musser. Family, friends and neighbors just could not believe the carnage that had taken place in such a small and welcoming community like Carthage.

Robert Stewart survived the shot to his chest and was charged with eight counts of first-degree murder but was sentenced to eight counts of second-degree murder. His defense claimed that he was under the influence of Ambien, a sleep aid, which lessened his control over his decision-making ability. The prosecutor argued that he knew exactly what he had been doing, presenting the fact that he had called several family members in the preceding days and told them that he had prostate cancer and was going to "go away." Friends who had seen him before the shooting testified to his depressed state. They argued that Robert had intended to go to Wanda's job and kill her and anyone else he could until the police killed him or he killed himself. In the end, he was sentenced to over 179 years in prison for his crime. He was truly the monster that for years parents in Carthage tried to tell their kids did not exist. He shattered the impression that things like that cannot happen in small-town America and brought the realization that evil can touch you wherever you are.

Chapter 17

TAR HEEL TRAGEDY

What is it that binds us to this place as to no other? It is not the well, or the bell, or the stone walls, or the crisp October nights or the memory of dogwoods blooming. No, our love for this place is based on the fact that it is as it was meant to be, the University of the people." Charles Kuralt knew what so many who have lived in Chapel Hill and gone to the University of North Carolina at Chapel Hill know. The town is the university, and the university is the town. Most people who have spent any amount of time there have left with a deep love and strong connection that lasts a lifetime. But even in this gorgeous southern sanctuary, madness and evil can penetrate the sheen of civility and beauty.

There, Wendall Williams carefully packed his backpack with hundreds of rounds of ammunition, rope and condoms. He threw on his green army coat that he had bought at a military surplus store and set out down Rosemary Street with his rifle. It was January 6, 1995, an overcast, gray day. He was on a mission to save the world, and the only way to do it was by killing everyone he saw. Passing cars and pedestrians became his focus as he walked down the street shooting. A young man ran up the stairs of a sorority house and was shot down on the steps. A bicyclist swerved to avoid the gunman but was shot down. The shooter came to the corner of Rosemary and Henderson and stopped to shoot at the back of the post office and anyone he saw in the vicinity. Rage and madness had overtaken him, and he had become death.

He had not always been a dangerous man. In high school, he was the captain of the swim team, the student body president and an Eagle Scout.

The Old Well on the campus of the University of North Carolina at Chapel Hill is a symbol of the peace and tranquility that is usually found on the campus and was shattered on a January morning in 1995. *Author's collection.*

He had graduated from the University of North Carolina at Chapel Hill and had moved on to the UNC Law School without setting off any alarms. But in law school, he began to act out in class and to claim, very loudly, that he had telepathic powers. He was arrested once by the campus police for yelling in a crowd and then punching himself in the face until officers could restrain him. After the incident, he was committed to a psychiatric hospital, where he told counselors that he was hearing voices from the "Thing," which was telling him to do things and putting horrific images in his head. Although he told them this and disclosed to them that he had a gun at his apartment, they released him anyway because they saw him as no threat to others.

The dean of students at the law school referred him to Student Services, where he began to see a psychiatrist, Dr. Myron Lipzin, who treated him and medicated him. Everyone who had experienced his outburst the previous school year agreed that the year following the beginning of the treatment, Wendell was doing well. It seemed with treatment he had turned a corner and was going to be all right, but then he received news that sent him into a downward spiral. Dr. Lipzin told him he was retiring and Wendell would need to continue his treatment with another doctor. They saw each other just six times before Lipzin retired. He was not formally referred to another doctor and was sent to another doctor by Student Services. Wendall's progress began to regress, and he stopped taking his medication. With Dr. Lipzin out of the picture, he would no longer go to his appointments with the new doctor. The "Thing" returned and told him that it was up to him to save the world. He had to do this by killing as many people as he saw. That January morning, he packed his bag, took his rifle and headed down Rosemary Street to obey his master.

He stopped shooting momentarily behind the post office and ducked into a doorway as police units began to arrive on the scene. He exchanged fire with them from the doorway, hitting one of the officers in the left hand. Nearby in the Tammany Hall Bar, Bill Leone heard shots being fired. He was a senior at Carolina and the manager of the bar. A former marine and Gulf War veteran, he moved toward the sound of the firing instinctively. Crawling through the gravel of the bar's parking lot, he came out behind Wendall. Wendall stepped out from the doorway again to engage the officers and was shot in the leg and knocked down. He regained his feet and staggered, still firing at the police. Leone saw his chance as Williamson stopped to reload his weapon. He charged him and tackled him just as he was turning to fire on him. He restrained Williamson until the police came over and arrested him.

When the shooting was over, Ralph Water Jr., a Chapel Hill resident, and Kevin Reinhardt, a student and lacrosse player, were dead. A campus police officer was wounded in the hand, and Bill Leone had been shot either by Williamson or by the police who were firing on Williamson at the time he tackled him. Another victim that day was the town of Chapel Hill. Although UNC is a large university, Chapel Hill is still a small town, and before that day, things like this just did not happen in a place like that. Reality settled over the town, and there was an unmistakable difference in the level of safety that students and residents felt.

Wendall Williamson was charged with two counts of first-degree murder but was found not guilty by reason of insanity. He was diagnosed with paranoid schizophrenia and committed to a mental hospital. In 1998, Williamson sued Dr. Lipzin because he said he should have been able to tell that he was dangerous and treated him further or referred him to another doctor. Dr. Lipzin had only met with him a half dozen times or so and had not met with him for eight months before the shooting. He argued that there was no way that he could have known Wendall was a danger to others and that his continued care after his retirement was not his responsibility. The jury agreed with Williamson and awarded him $500,000 in damages.

Williamson has written a book about his battle with mental health and what happened leading up to and the day of the shootings. He signed over the rights to a friend and set in motion actions that resulted in the Crime Victim's Compensation Act in North Carolina, which would prevent criminals from profiting from their crimes. Williamson has moved around from mental health facility to mental health facility over the years since he was committed. While at Dorothea Dix Hospital in Raleigh, he escaped and spent about five hours swimming in nearby Lake Wheeler until he got tired and called the hospital to come and pick him up.

Even though the safety of the picturesque town of Chapel Hill was shattered that day, residents pulled together as a community to heal. The night of the shooting, six hundred people gathered for a candlelight vigil at the site of the victims' deaths. Those involved have tried to move on as best they can, but the loss has been great. No matter how evil the act though, it could not kill the spirit of Chapel Hill or the university that bears its name. The memory is there but is drowned out by the unbreakable bond that people feel to the town and the school.

Chapter 18

THE GREENSBORO MASSACRE

"Death to the Klan! Death to the Klan! Death to the Klan!" Marchers of the Communist Workers' Party (CWP) chanted at the cars that drove back and forth in front of the Morningside housing project, where they had gathered to organize for the march they had planned. As the cars rolled slowly past, many carrying members of the Ku Klux Klan taunting them, the marchers chanted and hit the cars with their signs in defiance. As the situation reached a fever pitch of tension, a blue car stopped, and men got out. They walked around to the back of the car to the truck. As marchers confronted them, expecting a fistfight, the men produced guns and shots rang out. Chaos descended on the street as shots and screams engulfed the fall morning.

Greensboro was no stranger to marches and protests, having been a hot spot during the not so distant civil rights movement. A thriving textile city in the heart of the state, Greensboro had been the site of one of the most famous occurrences of the movement. After the Supreme Court's decision in *Brown v. Board of Education*, the South had to adjust to the new law of the land, which was integration. A few years later in Durham, several black men had gone to an ice cream parlor and demanded service in the whites-only section. They were refused, but their silent protest inspired other college students around the state and the South to take action. Later, four black students from North Carolina A&T University in Greensboro walked downtown to the Woolworth's and took a seat at the whites-only counter.

They demanded to be served and refused to leave without being afforded the same service that whites would receive. They were arrested, but the sit-in had an effect on the movement, and more and more nonviolent sit-ins began around the South.

By the 1970s, despite the many laws passed and the many progressions that had been made in the South and in North Carolina, black people still found themselves being discriminated against in many ways, including in the textile mills of Greensboro. An already hard environment where white workers also felt degraded and suffered from low wages and hard work, it was an attractive spot for labor organizers to flock to. The Communist Workers' Party was just such a group. Having come to Greensboro but not having any luck among white workers, the organization turned its attention to the mill's black employees. Party members came in and began to organize the workers while also speaking out against the racism that they were experiencing at work and in their community. The Communists saw an opportunity to sow discontent and get on the evening news by organizing a march, but it is doubtful they thought it would go so far.

On the morning of November 3, 1979, members of the Communist Workers' Party and local marchers began to form at the Morningside housing projects, where they were planning to start their march that would

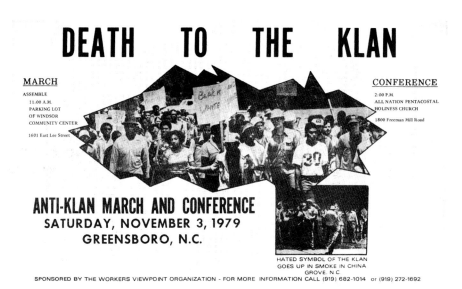

A flyer distributed by the Communist Workers' Party before the Death to the Klan march. *Courtesy of UNCG Library.*

go through town all the way down to city hall, where a rally would be held. They named the march the Death to the Klan march and had been putting out flyers saying that the Klan should be beaten out of Greensboro and that violence was the only language they understood. The CWP called for armed self-defense against the Klan and publicly called for the Klan members to show their faces at the march and face the wrath of the people. The Klan was listening and heard these provocations. They arrived at Morningside about forty strong, including Klansmen and members of the American Nazi Party. They came with intentions of answering the rhetoric with violence, and the situation soon escalated.

The sequence of events that happened next is unclear and a matter of great debate because things escalated so quickly. Many people say that the first shot was from a KKK member named Mark Sherer, who shot into the air and set off a barrage of fire from the Klan, Nazis and the few marchers who were themselves armed with handguns. The KKK members claim that they were fired on by one of the armed protestors and responded in self-defense. Whatever lit the fuse, the conflagration was short and bloody, with the marchers getting the worst of it by far. CWP members César Cuace, James Waller and Bill Sampson were killed almost immediately after the gunfire started. Marcher Sandi Smith, who had taken cover, was shot in the face as she peeked out to see what was going on and died on the spot. Eleven marchers were wounded, including Michael Nathan, who died later at the hospital. Much of the shootout was captured on the cameras of a local news station that had set up to cover the march. The footage played on the evening news that night, and the nation watched, horrified at the scene of violence and stunned at the carnage. The gunfight lasted just eighty-eight seconds but would have a deep effect on the community and the nation for years to come.

The police were criticized for the lack of speed with which they responded to the shooting. The Greensboro Police Department in 1979 was no stranger to marches and protests because of the heavy activity there during the civil rights movement. On November 3, there were only two GPD employees present. One was a detective, and another was a police photographer. They had been assigned to ride with the column of Klansmen and Nazis that had ridden into the marchers. They did not intervene when the shooting started, and by the time the police arrived in force, the shooters had escaped. It was discovered later that the Bureau of Alcohol, Tobacco and Firearms had an agent imbedded in the American Nazi Party and had been given a tip that there was violence planned for the march, but he had not reported the information to the local authorities.

In the state trial that followed, the prosecutors brought murder charges against five of the Klansmen: David Matthews, Jerry Smith, Jack Fowler, Harold Flowers and Billy Franklin. An all-white jury acquitted them of all charges one year after the shootings on the grounds of self-defense. Following the verdict, federal prosecutors charged nine men with civil rights violations in 1983. The following year, they were all acquitted once more, and the CWP and the marchers from the community in Greensboro felt that they had seen justice slip from their grasp. The tension in Greensboro only increased over the proceeding years, and the distrust between the black community and the police department continued to simmer. The Communist Workers' Party left with the mills that became dinosaurs and eventually became extinct as so many companies moved their manufacturing overseas.

The four white marchers were buried in Maplewood Cemetery, a predominantly black cemetery near the Morningside community. The body of Sandi Smith was sent back home to South Carolina at the request of her family. After a fight with city hall over political speech, a headstone monument was erected in Maplewood in remembrance of the dead. It reads:

Long Live the Communist Party 5

On November 3, 1979, the criminal monopoly capitalist class murdered Jim Waller, César Cuace, Mike Nathan, Bill Sampson, and Sandi Smith with government agents, Klan, and Nazis. Heroically defending the people, the 5 charged gunfire with bare fists and sticks. We vow this assassination will be the costliest mistake the capitalists have ever made, and the turning point of class struggle in the U.S.

The CWP 5 were among the strongest leaders of their times. Their deaths marked an end to capitalist stabilization (1950s–1970s) when American workers suffered untold misery, yet as a whole remained dormant for lack of its own leaders. In 1980 the deepest capitalist crisis began. The working class was awakening. The CWP 5 lived and died for all workers, minorities, and poor; for a world where exploitation and oppression will be eliminated, and all mankind freed; for the noble goal of communism. Their deaths, a tremendous loss to the CWP and to their families, are a clarion call to the U.S. people to fight for the workers' rule. In their footsteps waves of revolutionaries will rise and join our ranks.

We will overthrow the rule of the monopoly capitalist class! Victory will be ours!
November 3, 1980 Central Committee, CWP, USA

FIGHT FOR REVOLUTIONARY SOCIALISM AND WORKERS RULE.

It stands as a testament to the loss of civility and the ability to disagree without hatred and violence and reminds others of the consequences when groups of extremists collide.

Chapter 19
THE OUTLAWS

The rumble of the Harley-Davidson could be heard in the early morning darkness of July 4, 1979, along Allen Road South in Charlotte, North Carolina. William "Chains" Flamont, the president of the area chapter of the Outlaws Motorcycle Club, drew closer to the clubhouse. The house was a fortress with eight-foot walls surrounding, guard dogs and armed club members on guard around the clock. Lately, though, he felt the security had been lax. They had lost members recently to jail, and Chains felt that being shorthanded had caused them to take their foot off the gas and let their guards down. As he pulled into the driveway and around the house, he could see William "Water Head" Allen sitting on the porch. He scoffed with disgust as he looked at the young man leaned back with his leg propped up, obviously sleeping while he was supposed to be on guard. Water Head was a probationary member, and this was not going to help him get fully patched in. Chains knew Water Head was taking pain meds for his leg that had been injured, but he was still expected to stay awake on guard duty. As Chains walked up the stairs and prepared to scold him, he saw that he was not sleeping at all. He had been shot through the chest. His .38-caliber revolver lay unused on his lap. A Pabst Blue Ribbon beer sat on the floor by his chair, and a pack of Marlboros lay nearby.

Chains took out his own pistol and opened the door to the house, not knowing what to expect. On the floor he saw the dead body of William "Mouse" Dradenburg, blankets wrapped around his legs and lying close to his unused pistol. On the couch was Leonard "Terrible Terry" Henderson with his girlfriend, a seventeen-year-old runaway named Bridgette "Midget" Benfiled. Both had been shot dead where they lay. Across the room on the other couch was a stranger whom he did not recognize riddled with bullets from head to toe; he was later identified by dental records as Randell Feazel, who had most likely come to the clubhouse to get tattooed by Henderson. They were all dead, and their still bodies lay amid shell casings, trash and beer cans. Someone had taken them completely by surprise and murdered them in their sleep, giving them no time to defend themselves. When the police investigators came, Chains told them that he was sure it was the Hells Angels Motorcycle Club that they had been feuding with, but he had no information beyond that. There was a pay phone on the wall of the clubhouse that rang throughout the day as people learned of what had happened. The officers answered the calls, hoping to build a web of resources for the forthcoming investigation, but gleaned little information from them.

The Hells Angels and the Outlaws were products of the Second World War, when many veterans came back home and felt restless and misunderstood. Many of these men began to ride motorcycles, mostly Harley-Davidsons, and form motorcycle clubs where they could band together in a world where they felt so alone. The Outlaws Motorcycle Club had been formed before the war in 1936 but saw a large increase in membership as soldiers came home to find a slow-moving world that lacked danger or understanding for what we now would be able to diagnose as post-traumatic stress disorder. Over time, these early leaders began to shape these organizations into crime syndicates that were involved in everything from prostitution to drugs. In Charlotte by the 1970s, there were several motorcycle clubs operating in the area. Charlotte was a waystation in between Canada and Miami, and there was a steady stream of drugs moving back and forth. The Hells Angels, the Outlaws, the Tasmanian Devils and the Tar Heel Stompers vied for supremacy along this corridor and had turned many places around Charlotte into small war zones.

Considering the Hells Angels or any of the other clubs as prime suspects was a pretty safe bet for the Charlotte-Mecklenburg Police Department, but there were many questions the police had. First was how did someone get over the wall, past the dogs and sneak up on the guard without being noticed? Autopsies on the victims showed no signs of excessive alcohol or drugs in their systems, although it was obvious they had all been taken completely by surprise. After following the Hells Angels lead, it was determined that they were not involved. Tips soon turned to a known rabble-rouser named Gregory Scot "Teen Angel" Lindaman. He was a true biker and had seemed to grow up on two wheels. He was an expert mechanic who could take a bike apart and put it back together again. Once he had been a prospect with the Outlaws, but he had not made the cut. On the surface, he looked like a perfect fit, but he just could not get along with anyone in the club, so they let him go.

Lindaman was wanted on motorcycle theft in Charlotte at the time of the murders, and the police had him as a suspect for another murder that had taken place in December, that of a Tar Heel Stomper named Larry "Popeye" Pressley. Immediately after the murders on Allen Road, he skipped town. Less than two weeks later, he was picked up by the San Bernardino Police Department in California on the motorcycle theft warrant. He was sent back and questioned on the murders, which he swore he knew nothing about. He was cleared on the Popeye murder because witnesses claimed it was self-defense. Without evidence to hold him, they had to let him go. They picked up an associate of his named Andy Allan Pigg, but with no evidence and his refusal to cooperate, he had to be let go as well.

Many leads were followed, but nothing panned out for the CMPD. After many years, the case went cold but was never closed. The case was not closed until thirty-six years later, when information came from an anonymous source that the Charlotte-Mecklenburg Police Department will still not disclose. The source, which was deemed reliable, told them that the killers

Investigators search the outside of the Outlaw MC Clubhouse after the bodies of several members were discovered inside. *Courtesy of the Charlotte-Mecklenburg Police Department.*

were in fact Lindaman and Pigg. Apparently, Lindaman had a confrontation with Terrible Terry and had been booted from the club. He carried the resentment with him and planned to settle the score. The source claimed that they shot Water Head over the wall with a .223-caliber rifle while he sat on the porch. Moving quickly over the wall, they came into the house guns blazing, shooting everyone there with 9mm pistols.

It all lined up with the evidence that had been compiled at the scene, and the police were certain that the tipster was right about what happened. The problem they had when they confirmed the evidence was that both Lindaman and Pigg were long since dead. Lindaman was killed in a car crash in Houston, Texas, in 1990. Pigg settled down in Charlotte and opened a welding shop. He died in 2007 in his home of liver disease. Although the case has been closed, it can never be known for sure what happened that night now that everyone who was there is gone, but the evidence has given some closure to families and also to the investigators who worked on the case for years.

Chapter 20

THE VALENTINE'S DAY MURDERS

It was a cool, sunny day in late February when a surveyor parked his truck on Howe Street in Orange County. Fumbling with his equipment, he stepped off the dirt and gravel road into the leaves and began to walk into the woods to begin his survey of the land around Cabe's Landing on the Eno River. He had not taken many steps into the woods when he noticed what he thought was a mannequin's leg sticking out from the leaves beside a tree. It had to be a mannequin's leg, he thought as he walked over to it, because it was snow white. But as he came closer, he realized that he was wrong. As he neared the tree, he saw the bodies of a man and a woman slumped over, leaning against each other. Their hands were tied behind their backs with rope, and they had rope tied around their necks that was attached to the tree. The leaves and branches from the tree had fallen on them and partially covered their young bodies.

He stumbled back, dropping his equipment and running back to his truck. When the Orange County Sheriff's Department arrived, they noticed some very disturbing things about the crime scene. Both the man and the woman were fully clothed, and there was no sign of any kind of sexual abuse. The ropes tied around their necks were tied tightly to the tree, and there were multiple strangulation wounds on their necks. This indicated that they had been pulled tightly to the tree, strangling them, but then the ropes had been loosened before it killed them, only to be pulled back and strangled again. This had been done over and over, obviously for the purpose of torturing the two. There were deep ruts in the ground around the tree, showing how they had struggled against the strangling. The only difference in the condition of the bodies was that the liver of the young woman had a tear in it. It is believed that it came from a punch to the abdomen by the killer. This was the only indication that the perpetrator of this crime had treated them differently. Although there were many questions investigators had, they would soon find out the names of this unlucky couple. The answer would come from nearby Durham, North Carolina.

Watts Hospital was opened in 1895 as Durham's first hospital. Serving white men and women only, the hospital grew and expanded as the premier option in Durham for healthcare for many years until the opening of Duke Hospital. The African American community relied on Lincoln Hospital, which was an all-black facility, up until 1964 when Watts integrated. By 1971, the hospital was still in operation but had seen more prosperous days. One of the highlights of the hospital remained the Watts School of Nursing, which operated on the grounds. Young women had studied and trained alongside experienced doctors and nurses here since the hospital's opening, and the school had a great reputation. One of the students there in 1971 was a twenty-year-old young lady from Sanford, North Carolina, named Patricia Mann. She was known as a really good girl who was very bright and loved by all who knew her. She was dating a tall, handsome nineteen-year-old named Jesse McBane from Pittsboro, North Carolina, who went to North Carolina State University in Raleigh.

They had been dating for a while, and those who knew them could see the affection they had for each other. On Valentine's Day 1971, Jesse came to Watts to escort Patricia to the dance the hospital was having for the nurses and staff. They danced to Tony Orlando and Dawn and the Carpenters, laughing and having a great time. After the dance, Patricia signed out at her dorm, letting them know that she would be back by the 1:00 a.m. curfew. No one saw her alive again. The next morning, when her friends realized she had not come home the night before, they were immediately worried. She was a rule follower if nothing else, and they could not imagine her not obeying curfew unless something bad had happened. They called the police, who were not as concerned as they were. Generally, they did not begin to search for anyone unless they had been missing for at least twenty-four hours, but they said they would take a look around.

Later that day, Jesse's car was found by some of Patricia's friends who had been looking for her parked on a lover's lane near the Hillandale Golf Course off Medford Road. It was a common spot for local young people to

Watts Hospital was Durham's first hospital and housed the prestigious Watts School of Nursing, where Patricia Mann and Jesse McBane disappeared. *Author's collection.*

go for privacy. This lover's lane area was not one of the regular places that Patricia and Jesse were known to go. Patricia's roommates had checked all of those places and found no signs of them. When the car was found, it was locked and totally undisturbed. There was no sign of Jesse or Patricia and no indications of any kind of struggle. It became a missing persons case for the next two weeks until the survey worker happened upon the bodies just a few miles away in Orange County.

The Orange County Sheriff's Department and the Durham County Sheriff's Department worked together on the case to try to assemble the pieces of the puzzle, but much remained a mystery. They appeared to have been kidnapped from their car on Medford Road without a struggle. The manner in which they were killed had been brutal and torturous. The killer had wanted them to suffer greatly. The tear in Patricia's liver seemed to indicate that she had either struggled with the killer and been struck or that the killer had targeted her with his anger for a personal reason. The investigators had few leads, and there was just so little evidence that it quickly became a cold case. Their inclination was that it was someone who

The pond near Medford Road where McBane's car was found. *Courtesy of William Jackson.*

The woods where the bodies of young lovers Patricia Mann and Jesse McBane were found. *Courtesy of William Jackson.*

had known Patricia and had possibly committed the crime as a crime of passion. The strongest evidence pointed to a doctor at Watts Hospital who was very wealthy and influential, but officers could not compile enough evidence to charge him.

Today, the tragedy remains unsolved, but the families of the two young people who had their precious lives taken so many years ago have not forgotten. They have kept the case open by continually writing letters and following leads themselves. The sheriff in Orange County recently commented on the murders to a local news reporter. He stated that the evidence pointed to one individual, but he had refused to cooperate in any way. He refused to take a polygraph exam or provide a DNA sample. The sheriff hoped that one day they would have the evidence necessary to legally compel the suspect to cooperate, but for now, they are still working the case from every angle possible. Maybe one day justice, though delayed, will be served for this young couple and their families. Hopefully one day, they will be able to rest on the fact that the monster who took their daughter and son has been caught.

THE COASTAL PLAIN

To the east of the Piedmont, the land begins to flatten and turn into rolling fields of tobacco and other crops. Highways and roads snake through small towns on the way to some of the most gorgeous beaches in the United States, from the Outer Banks of the north shore, where horses run wild at Corolla, to the bustling beach towns in the south, where during the summer it seems the party never stops. After the sunshine fades and the air turns colder, these beaches become empty and quiet, but the beauty remains all year long. It would be easy to forget that just as the seasons change here, so does the forever marching of time. Good things and bad things happen here just like anywhere else, and sadly, the Coastal Plain has had its share of sorrow at places like Fort Bragg, where young men and women who train to fight for freedom overseas faced death from a fellow soldier, and Windsor, where good people who just wanted to live their lives were slaughtered for being in the wrong place at the wrong time.

Eastern North Carolina is a place where people come from around the United States for vacation and recreation, but tragedy has also visited this beautiful place many times. *Author's collection.*

Chapter 21

THE REVEREND CARAWAN

Schoolmaster Clement Lassiter knew he had to walk past Reverend Carawan's house to get from the schoolhouse on Rose Bay to his next teaching assignment on Lake Matamuskeet, but it was not until the last moment that he decided to cut through the woods to save some time. Or maybe he wanted the concealment of the woods to save him from a confrontation on the road with Reverend Carawan. As he walked among the trees, he realized he had a pit in his stomach and his heart was beating at a faster pace. He stopped and leaned against a tree and closed his eyes to calm himself. "No need to be so nervous," he thought. He took off his hat, wiped the sweat from his brow and ran his hand through his hair. Suddenly, he heard the snap of a branch close behind him, and he turned to see the Reverend George Carawan standing just a few feet from him. He was holding a shotgun and looked upon Lassiter with an expressionless face. The schoolmaster turned and faced him. He was nervous and tried to bring a smile to his face. "You scared me, Reverend," he said. George Carawan raised his shotgun and fired right into Lassiter's chest. With that, the very esteemed Reverend George Washington Carawan of Hyde County, North Carolina, sealed his fate and let the world see without question the wickedness that had been hidden within him for years.

Today, Hyde County, North Carolina, is a sedate and peaceful place, as it has always been. It is one of the largest counties in North Carolina by area and yet one of the least populated. However, it was there that, in 1800, a boy was born who would rise to prominence and then fall hard from grace. He was George Washington Carawan. Four years after his birth, his father passed away, leaving his mother alone with young George, his brother and his sister.

His mother was a cold and hard woman. She had a reputation as a woman who could take care of herself and her own and also as a woman who was prone to violent mood swings. She insisted on her children being highly disciplined, and she ensured that they would have the best religious education possible in Hyde County. She was a member of the Old School Baptist Church and made sure that she and the children were there each service. She tried her best to make sure that the children grew up with a reverence for God, but in the case of young George, it would just not stick.

He was a very smart boy. He was described by neighbors as "a wild boy given to profane swearing, confounding right and wrong, and making jest of religion and its professors." All those years in church had not totally been for naught though. George had a vast knowledge of the scripture and used it frequently to baffle preachers from both the Baptist church and the Methodist church. If he heard preaching, he came running so that he could confront and argue with the preacher. He was known for picking out a characteristic of a minister who was passing through town and imitating him while giving mock sermons. The sermons were so good that it would stand to make people think how the minister could be delivering a God-inspired sermon if George could give an equally impactful sermon as a farce.

Around the age of twenty-one, George married Elizabeth Carrow and moved to Goose Creek Island in Beaufort County, North Carolina. His brother was a preacher there at Goose Creek Church, and George lived nearby, where he kept a small farm. He attended his brother's church and tended his farm. Life was good. He lived there for about four years and then left to move back to Hyde County, claiming an inappropriate relationship had taken place between his brother and his wife. They packed up and moved back to Lake Matamuskeet, where he settled back on the family farm.

George Carawan was known far and wide as a rotten man until the year 1827, when he miraculously experienced a religious conversion. He joined the South Matamuskeet Baptist Church and was baptized by the church elders. As he was baptized, the elder performing the ceremony proclaimed that George Carawan was a great man of God and would do great things in God's service. He was thought to be prophetic for a long time because, sure enough, George soon became a minister of the gospel after claiming that he had a vision in the night of Christ standing beside his bed holding a scroll with a great glowing halo of the Holy Spirit surrounding him. He told him to "go forth and preach the gospel." The now Reverend Carawan moved his family once more to the head of the lake and began to preach the gospel.

His reputation changed from a rotten and vile individual to a man on fire for God. He preached at churches across Carteret County, even taking over his brother's church at Goose Creek after he died. He spent the next twenty years as the head pastor of the Lake Matamuskeet Church and held sway over most of the Baptist churches in the region. The conversions and baptisms he performed were counted in the hundreds. He took no pay for his work. During this time, he was a successful farmer and businessman, and

The Reverend George W. Carawan. *Courtesy of the Harvard Library.*

many saw this as a blessing from God for the giving that he did through his ministry. The Lord was taking care of the shepherd who was taking care of his flock. As a pastor, he was very strict in the implementation of God's laws and church rules. This made him an enemy of many men at the time because of his harsh demeanor and his success.

Although he had become a changed man in the view of the majority of the good people of Hyde County, he still had a violent, dark cloud hanging over him that most could not see. Although hidden from public view, his wife saw it daily. Carawan beat her regularly and for the slightest offense, constantly concocting reasons that she deserved a beating, like contrived affairs with other men. In 1839, Elizabeth Carawan passed away, and he remarried within three weeks to a woman named Mary Bell. This caused a stir in the knitting circles, but it did not do enough damage to his reputation to cause him to lose stature in the community. Mary suffered from the same beatings as Elizabeth did but was ever the faithful wife.

During his marriage to Mary, he became involved with a young girl living in his home as a house girl. Her name was Polly Richards, and she was a beautiful girl. One day, the reverend began to ask young men in town to marry her. She was pretty enough, but it was sudden, and he could find no takers. He finally settled on a seventeen-year-old boy named Hudson who was known as being mentally slow. He married them himself and set them on their way. The community was confused and shocked at the suddenness of the nuptials and the push that the reverend had put on the relationship. Things began to become clear to the parish when the boy took sick just a few weeks later and suddenly died. Just a few days later, the community became aware that Polly was pregnant. Rumors began to spread about Carawan, and he was dismissed from his church, but after much repentance, he was able to convince the elders and the congregation of his penance and regain his position.

The reverend was always one step ahead of his reputation, it seems, until his luck finally ran out in 1852 when he took on a quiet young teacher as a boarder. Clement Lassiter was loved by his students and other members of the community universally and was known as a good and honest young man. One night at the Carawan house, the reverend began to beat his wife in Lassiter's presence. Lassiter intervened to stop the beating, and Carawan turned on him in a fit of hot rage. The teacher pulled a knife on the reverend and the fight was averted, but he was kicked out of the Carawan house and had to find a new place to board.

Carawan was a vindictive man, and he took his wife to the magistrate and made her claim that Lassiter had raped her while living there. It was obvious to the magistrate that it was fabricated and forced, and he would not accept the accusation because he did not want Mrs. Carawan to possibly perjure herself. Nevertheless, the rumor began to spread that Lassiter had been intimate with Mrs. Carawan while living in the home, and the teacher eventually sued the reverend for slander. Lassiter began to live in fear in the community and communicated it to the new family he was boarding with. He was especially wary of walking past the Carawan house on his way to teach at the Lake Matamuskeet schoolhouse.

One fateful day in November, Lassiter set out along the road to Lake Matamuskeet to teach. He was seen by many neighbors along the way, but he never made it to the schoolhouse. A few days later, his body was found buried in a shallow grave off the road. It is said that when the news of his body being found reached the good reverend, he told his wife that he had to leave town or he would be hanged for sure. He traveled across North Carolina and into Tennessee to hide out under an alias. He was depending on remaining friends to sell his property and send him money, but they refused, and after a few months, he had to sneak back into Hyde County to try to sell the goods himself.

His slave Seth spotted him as he tried to come back to his house to see his family. Seth immediately ran and told the sheriff. Carawan was arrested and put on trial for the murder of Clement Lassiter. It was against the law for slaves to testify against their masters, but Seth told the authorities that he had been made to go with Reverend Carawan and bury the body of Lassiter. The trial was very contentious, with the lawyers for the defendant challenging every point the prosecution made. Without Seth's testimony, the evidence was circumstantial at best. The night before the verdict, Carawan was allowed to have visitors and got the chance to see his family one last time before his judgment.

Despite the lack of concrete evidence, the jury found Reverend Carawan guilty of murder. Upon hearing the verdict, he rose to his feet and reached into his coat, producing a pistol. He aimed and fired at the prosecutor, hitting him in the heart and killing him. The deputies tried to restrain him, but he was able to pull another pistol out of his coat and shoot himself in the head. As the people of the court screamed and jostled to either flee or get a closer look at the tussle, the reverend died there on the courtroom floor. It is believed that one of his visitors the night before had provided him with the pistols. There on the courtroom floor, he was exposed as the monster that he was.

Chapter 22
MARSHALL "CARBINE" WILLIAMS

The murder of a deputy in the backwoods of Cumberland County, North Carolina, put in jail a man who would gain fame while behind bars and change the course of the history of firearms and also warfare. He would make such an impact that he would be set free to do his work by the governor of North Carolina, become a celebrity and be portrayed on the silver screen by one of the most famous actors who has ever lived. Even so, it was a troubled life despite his freedom, and the question that haunted the family of the deputy remained, "Was justice served"?

On the morning of July 21, 1921, Cumberland County sheriff N.H. Greachy, along with five of his deputies, crept through the woods near Godwin, North Carolina, looking for a still. They had been tipped off about the location and had been told who was running the illegal operation. As they got closer to the camp, they could hear talking, and the still began to come into view between the trees and foliage. They heard a shout followed by running as the men noticed them and scattered. Greachy stepped into the clearing and found exactly what he had been looking for: a large copper pot with tubes and barrels scattered around a roaring fire by a stream. He set his deputies to destroying the liquor and carrying the evidence out of the woods. He would need it. The bootlegger was Marshall David Williams, a well-off son of a landowner in Cumberland County. The sheriff knew he would be in for a fight when it went to court.

The deputies carried the large copper pot out of the woods along with smaller items and loaded them into the back seat of the car. The cars were loaded down, and the deputies were unable to fit for the drive back into town. Sixty-three-year-old deputy Alfred Pate, a twenty-year veteran of the sheriff's department, volunteered to ride back on the running board as they made their way down the country road they had parked on before they entered the woods. As the cars moved along the road, shots rang out from the woods. Deputy Pate was struck twice and fell from the side of the car, dead. Other deputies leapt from their cars to return fire, but the attackers had once again fled into the woods. There was little doubt who the shooter was.

Marshall David Williams was born on November 13, 1900, in Cumberland County. He was the eldest of seven children; his father had five additional children from his first marriage. Williams's father was a very wealthy landowner around Godwin, where he owned several hundred acres. Marshall was always mischievous and in trouble constantly as a child. He was expelled from school in the eighth grade and made to work full time on his father's farm. When he was fifteen, he lied about his age and joined the United States Navy. They soon discovered the lie and sent him back home to Godwin. At seventeen, he was enrolled in Blackstone Military Academy in Virginia in hopes of straightening him out, but he was expelled before his first year was completed for stealing. He was found with rifles and ammunition from the academy's armory in the trunk of his car and was once again sent home to Godwin.

In 1918, he married Margaret Cooke, with whom he would have a son, and took a job at the Atlantic Coast Line Railroad as a laborer. He was seemingly on the right track and appeared to be settling down until one day on the job, he pulled a pistol and shot at a bird that was flying by. Marsh, as his friends called him, found himself once again excused from a job and rejected for his behavior. He slinked back to his father and once again was put to work on the farm. He found the need for more money and more excitement, so he hired several local black men and set up a still in the woods, where he began to make moonshine whiskey. He was in the bootlegging business now and had no idea how his newest enterprise would change his life and change the course of the history of firearms around the world.

After the murder of Deputy Pate, the sheriff arrested Marsh Williams and charged him with first-degree murder. His father hired him a lawyer, and he entered a plea of not guilty due to insanity. He was identified by the deputies who were at the scene and also by the men who had been working at the still with him. On the advice of his attorney, he pulled the plea of not guilty and entered a plea of guilty for second-degree murder. Williams was sentenced

David Marshall "Carbine" Williams and his wife before the murder of Deputy Pate. *Courtesy of the North Carolina State Archives, Raleigh, NC.*

to thirty years of hard labor at Caledonia State Prison in Halifax County, North Carolina, which was known as a hard prison.

In prison, he worked in the machine shop and seemed to finally find a place where he could focus and steady his erratic behavior. He had been designing his own firearms since childhood, when he would use wood and nails to make some form of gun. Working in the machine shop, he had access to many tools and materials that he had never worked with before, and he began to dream about various designs of firearms. He began to draw out plans on materials brought to him by his family when they visited, and over time, he began to work on the prison guards' weapons for them instead of them having to go to a gunsmith. Williams developed deep trust with the guards and the warden, so much so that they allowed him to eventually begin to work on creating his firearm designs in the prison's machine shop without having to sneak around. While in prison, he developed a gas-operated floating chamber that allowed firearms to use small-caliber rounds as well as the rounds the weapon was intended to fire. He was unable to patent this new technology while he was in prison, but gun makers and the War Department took notice.

Williams continued his work and became a model prisoner at Caledonia. His family began to petition the governor for a commutation due to his behavior in prison and the work he was doing with firearms. On December 16, 1927, Governor Angus McClean reduced his sentence from thirty years to twenty years, and Williams was released from prison on September 29, 1929. He went back home to Cumberland County and resumed the work he had begun in prison of making and innovating firearms.

After prison, he worked for Colt, Remington, Winchester and the War Department. He patented many of his innovations and helped the United States prepare for war by making it possible for soldiers to train with weapons that they would be using in combat but shooting smaller and cheaper live rounds for practice. This saved millions of dollars and countless lives when the Second World War came. Williams helped develop a smaller, more compact rifle that was easier to be handled by support personnel, rear echelon troops and special operations soldiers. It was called the carbine, and Williams became known to history as "Carbine" Williams thereafter. In 1952, after the impact of his contributions was felt, MGM released the movie *Carbine Williams* starring Jimmy Stewart in the lead role.

Carbine Williams spent the rest of his life dealing with fame and a drinking problem. In the 1960s, his health began to deteriorate, and by 1972, he was admitted to Dorothea Dix Mental Hospital in Raleigh, North Carolina. He

Above: Carbine Williams Workshop. *Courtesy of the North Carolina State Archives, Raleigh, NC.*

Left: Williams found fame after his release from prison but never truly escaped his demons. *Courtesy of the North Carolina State Archives, Raleigh, NC.*

died there on January 8, 1975, due to pneumonia. Carbine Williams began his life as a troubled young man and graduated to murder at a young age, yet somewhere in his first few years at Caledonia, he decided that he had to change. His second chance and contributions to the Allied victory in the Second World War are a testament to anyone who has made a mistake and wants to turn his life around—although these good deeds that Williams did in the second act of his life would be little comfort to the loved ones of Deputy Alfred Pate. Deputy Pate didn't have the chance for a do-over of his life, and no matter what contributions Williams made, he is still responsible for taking the life of a good man.

Chapter 23
THE SEVEN BRIDGES KILLER

Interstate 95 runs along the Eastern Seaboard of the United States from Maine all the way down to Florida. It passes through some of the biggest cities in the nation like Boston, New York, Baltimore, Washington, D.C., Richmond and Miami. Along the way, not long after you enter North Carolina from Virginia heading south, I-95 runs directly to the west of Rocky Mount. Founded on the Tar River, Rocky Mount has always been a blue-collar town focused on textiles and crowded with mills. After the Civil War, Rocky Mount also became a hub for tobacco farmers to sell their crops. A mix of urban millworkers and farmers gave the town an identity that was unique even among other small towns in North Carolina. Times have changed in North Carolina, and textiles and tobacco have both experienced declines and have left Rocky Mount struggling to find another industry to support its population. The last few decades have brought an epidemic to the east side of Rocky Mount in the form of drugs and prostitution. Many young girls have been caught up in a life of danger and sadness because of their addiction to crack and the dangerous methods by which they earn the money to acquire drugs.

Living a life outside the law creates a perfect storm for predators. Many girls in Rocky Mount who became addicted to drugs turned to prostitution as a means to earn the money needed to satisfy their addictions. Working the streets on the east side of the city often made them easy prey for men with bad intentions. It was not strange for prostitutes to be beaten or raped by men, and because of the nature of their association, the girls felt helpless to report any of these crimes to the authorities. Between 2004 and 2010, a dozen girls or more went missing on the east side of Rocky Mount. Wayward girls in low-income and high-crime areas are not always easy for the police to track, and many times it is assumed that they have just run off or disappeared. Frustrated family members wait, sometimes forever, to find out what happened to their girls.

The first body of one of these girls was found in 2005. Melody Wiggins was found near Noble Pond Road just south of Highway 64. Her body was partially clothed and was decomposing. She had been struck in the head and had multiple stab wounds. The second body was found behind a home on Seven Bridges Road in 2007 and was in a similar state of decomposition, with similar wounds. The body was identified as a young woman named Jackie "Nikki" Thorpe. The next body was discovered by a farmer working on a fence near Seven Bridges Road in 2008 just north of Rocky Mount. He was overcome by a horrible smell while taking down a section of electric fence and moved closer to what he thought was a dead deer. He stepped back in horror when he realized it was the remains of a woman, facedown, naked and decomposing, with her hands raised above her head as if waving for help. She was identified as Ernestine Battle, a fifty-year-old woman who, like the first two victims, was known by police to work the streets in Rocky Mount at night.

Despite the missing girls and the remains that had been found, local authorities did not have any indication of the killer's identity or even that they were dealing with a serial killer. The pieces of the puzzle did not begin to assemble for police until March 2009, when a body was found by some local boys riding all-terrain vehicles in the woods. She fit the same profile as the other women who had been found. She was strangled and struck in the head, partially decomposed and had been dumped in the same area. She was identified as twenty-eight-year old Tarsha Nicholson. The police were able to extract DNA from her remains and also were able to link the location of her body to a strange arrest that had taken place near the location around the time of her disappearance.

Two months before she had been found, and the last day Tarsha was seen by her family, Antwan Pittman had been arrested just two hundred yards from where her body was found. When he was arrested, he was wearing muddy boots and his pants were hanging open. Pittman was a registered sex offender and known by the local police. He had been convicted of sexually assaulting a two-year-old in 1992 and had accumulated a rap sheet that spanned a wide range of offensives, from assault to resisting arrest. He had been hiding in plain sight in front of everyone's eyes for years, and although he was on the Rocky Mount Police Department radar as someone they had to watch, they never would have guessed he would turn out to be a serial killer.

The police were able to identify his semen in Tarsha's body through DNA examination and connected the proximity of the arrest and the date of her disappearance. They decided they needed to bring Pittman in for questioning. He had been working at a chicken processing plant at the time and told the police that he had never hired a prostitute in his life and had no idea who she was when shown pictures of Ms. Nicholson. When he was presented the DNA evidence that he had, in fact, had intercourse with her, he changed his story. He then claimed that he had been flagged down by her and offered sex for money. He said he had taken her to a motel that charged hourly rates, had sex with her once and dropped her off near a library in town. The police did not buy his story, and he was arrested for murder.

There were just too many reasons to believe the evidence the prosecutor had against him and no reason to take Antwan Pittman's word for anything. The jury took less than one hour to convict him to life in prison. After the verdict was read, Pittman sobbed and cried out, "You all are sending an innocent man to prison for life! I did not kill that woman!" Although the police and prosecutor have strong feelings that he was responsible for the other deaths, he has never admitted to them, and they lack the DNA evidence with the other murders that they had with Tarsha Nicholson. In 2010, another body was found, this time of a woman named Roberta Williams, which was decomposing in the same area.

The fact that Pittman was only charged with the one murder has left a wound for the families of the other victims that will never heal. Although it is assumed that Antwan Pittman was the Seven Bridges Killer, there will probably never be closure or certainty. Prosecutors have put him behind bars for the rest of his life for the death of one of the girls, but many in the community desire the investigation continue to prove his responsibility for the other murders. Girls still go missing sometimes from the east side of Rocky Mount, but no more bodies have been found. Have they just disappeared into the underworld of drugs and prostitution, or is there still a killer on the loose who has become better at concealing his crimes? Is the Seven Bridges Killer still hiding in plain sight?

Chapter 24

BETRAYAL

Neal Henderson nervously gripped the steering wheel of the borrowed Ford Mustang alone in the dark. Windows down to stave off the humid Washington, North Carolina night, he could hear the crickets chirping all around him. He felt alone and vulnerable waiting for the deed to be done. After about half an hour, he couldn't wait any longer and pulled the car out of his hiding spot and drove closer to the subdivision where his accomplice had gone. He cruised slowly, looking for his confederate, but he wasn't where he was supposed to be. He could hear his heart beating in his chest, and he felt that he had been waiting for hours although it was actually just a few minutes before he heard him coming. Footsteps beat a rhythm through the night running toward the car on the blacktop, and then Henderson saw him. James Upchurch appeared out of the night and jumped into the passenger's seat. His chest heaved and he said, "I did it! I can't believe I did it! I never want to see that much blood again the rest of my life. Let's get out of here!" Henderson pulled off, and they drove to a dark place off the main road in a tobacco field. Upchurch changed clothes and threw the old clothes, a knife and some maps on the ground. They poured gas on the pile and lit a match, and as the flames licked over the evidence, they drove away, heading back to Raleigh. As they drove, they sat in silence, wondering if they had just committed the perfect crime.

Leith von Stein married Bonnie Pritchard in 1979 and with her had inherited a ready-made family of a new wife and her two pre-teen children, Angela and Chris. In 1987, Leith's parents died and left him a handsome inheritance of over $1 million. He and Bonnie had plans to spend their time managing their wealth and living the good life. There was really only one thing that was straining their relationship during this time. Chris had graduated from high school that year and gone off to North Carolina State University in Raleigh. He had started out strong but had slipped in the second semester. Between the end of the school year and summer school, he started hanging out with some guys around his age named Neal and James. They played Dungeons and Dragons, the role-play fantasy game; smoked pot; and drank most of the time. Chris developed a very adversarial relationship with his mother and stepfather during this time, as Leith disapproved of how Chris was wasting his time and their money at State. The tension was so high between them that on a visit that summer, Chris and Leith had almost come to blows after a heated argument over dinner.

Chris went back to Raleigh and enrolled in a second summer session, where he fell back in with Henderson and Upchurch. Pritchard began to talk to them about what life would be like if his parents were gone. He talked of the money he would inherit and how they could live like kings, drinking and smoking pot all day every day and playing Dungeons and Dragons all they wanted without having to worry about anything. The talk began to turn serious, and they began to formulate plans on how to kill them. They discussed putting sleeping pills in their food and setting the house on fire, but the plan did not pan out. Finally, they devised a plan they were confident would work. Henderson and Upchurch would take Pritchard's car, leaving him in Raleigh to establish an alibi. They would drive to Washington, fake a break-in and murder Leith and Bonnie in their sleep. Chris Pritchard drew out a map of the neighborhood and a floor plan of the house they lived in at 110 Lawson Road.

On Sunday, July 24, 1988, Henderson and Upchurch drove to Washington, leaving Pritchard behind as planned. They drove around the neighborhood, looking for a good place to park, and Upchurch told Henderson to park and wait for him. Leith and Bonnie had gone to dinner that night and came home at about 11:00 p.m. They went to their bedroom and were asleep by midnight, not knowing the terror that was descending upon them. Bonnie was suddenly awakened by screams from Leith lying next to her. She could see the silhouette of a figure wielding a club or some other type of weapon. Paralyzed with fear, she watched as the figure turned on her and began to strike. When she regained consciousness, she reached for Leith and felt that his hand was limp. She began to worry about Angela, who had been listening to her stereo in her room when they had gone to bed. Bonnie managed to call 911 and get the police on the way to the house, unable to move and afraid the attacker might still be in the house.

As Henderson and Upchurch were washing the car of mud and filling up the tank for the journey back to Raleigh at a gas station outside town, officers from the Washington Police Department were responding to the calls of a home invasion and attack on Lawson Road. The responding officers found a broken window by the back door and, upon searching the house, found Bonnie and Leith in the bedroom covered with blood. Bonnie was in critical condition, and Leith was already dead. Bonnie told the officers through strained breaths that her daughter was in the room across the hall. The officers moved toward the door of Angela's room, expecting the worst, but when they opened her door, they found her unharmed and sleeping. They called Chris at college, and he pretended to be totally upset, even calling the campus police and having an officer drive him to Washington because he said he could not find his car.

Bonnie remained in critical condition for some time, and Chris began a months-long campaign of lies trying to keep his secret from his family. The police had found the partially burned remains of a shoe, a knife and a map—evidence that they were able to link back to Chris Pritchard. He was arrested in June 1989, to the surprise of his mother, who had been his biggest defender over the preceding months as the police began to question him. By December, he had confessed to the whole thing. Neal Henderson had also been arrested in June and had been cooperating with the police. Henderson and Pritchard both laid the majority of the blame, including the actual murder, on Upchurch. The testimony of Pritchard and Henderson and the physical evidence that the police had gathered doomed James Upchurch, who was convicted of murder and sentenced to death. He was later resentenced to life in prison because the original verdict was thrown out on procedural matters from the first trial. Henderson was convicted of murder in the second degree and aiding and abetting assault with intent to kill. He received a forty-year sentence for Leith and a six-year sentence for Bonnie but was paroled in 2000. Chris Pritchard was convicted of aiding and abetting second-degree murder and was sentenced to life in prison for Leith and twenty years for Bonnie. He was paroled in 2007.

The murder of Leith von Stein was hard for the small town of Washington to deal with. The implications of a son plotting to kill his own mother and stepfather for financial gain went against all of the values the people of Washington held dear. The murder also gained national attention and brought negative attention to the role-playing game Dungeons and Dragons, which was a large part of Pritchard, Henderson and Upchurch's interactions with one another leading up to the murder. It was speculated that they went too deep into the fantasy world and lost sight of real-world consequences and repercussions. There is no way to know for sure the true impact of the game, but the betrayal of Chris Pritchard against his mother was complete and unquestionable. Bonnie von Stein was able to forgive her son despite his actions and stood by him throughout his incarceration. When he got out, she was there to take care of him and try to help him reenter society. Pritchard became a born-again Christian and often speaks of forgiveness in churches across eastern North Carolina.

Chapter 25
THE BALLAD OF THE GREEN BERET DOCTOR

There was rarely a finer-looking couple than Jeffrey and Colette MacDonald. Jeffrey was the captain of the football team, senior class president and voted both most likely to succeed and most popular. He married his high school sweetheart, Colette Stevenson, in 1964. She was a beauty and followed Jeffrey to Princeton and then went on with him to Northwestern University for medical school. After his internship, he joined the United States Army and tried out for the Green Berets. He was accepted and stationed at Fort Bragg in Fayetteville, North Carolina. By the time the MacDonald family arrived at Fort Bragg, it had grown. Jeffrey and Colette were the parents of two precious girls named Kimberly and Kristen. Fayetteville in the 1960s was a wild place. Soldiers coming home from Vietnam mixed with hippies and drug dealers and those new recruits who were just preparing to go to Vietnam. Tension between the town's population and the army was palpable, and Dr. MacDonald often found himself having to report soldiers to their superiors for drug use. But within this storm of turmoil, the MacDonalds looked like the picture-perfect American family.

On the rainy morning of February 17, 1970, telephone operators at Fort Bragg received a call reporting a stabbing at 544 Castle Drive. When the military police arrived, they found the house dark and quiet. The front door was locked, and when no one answered, they sent an MP around to check the back door. He found it open, and upon entering the house, he found a gruesome sight. Jeffrey MacDonald was lying facedown with his arm wrapped over Colette in their bedroom. She had been stabbed several times with a knife and an icepick and was covered with blood. She had two broken arms from defending herself from strikes with a blunt object. The word "pig" was written in blood on the headboard. Five-year-old Kimberly was in her bed, stabbed in the neck and clubbed to death. Kristen was also dead in her bed at two years old, stabbed over thirty times with a knife and over a dozen times with an icepick. Jeffrey MacDonald was not as injured as the rest of his family. He was alive and was taken to Womack Army Hospital. He had bruises and cuts on his face and chest and a stab wound on his torso, which had caused one of his lungs to collapse.

When the military police investigators questioned MacDonald in the hospital, he told them he had fallen asleep on the couch on the night of February 16 and had been awakened by the screams of his wife and daughter Kimberly. He claimed that he sat up on the couch and was attacked by three males, one black and two white, with an icepick, a club and a knife. He told the investigators that there was also a woman with blond hair and a large floppy white hat holding a candle chanting, "Acid is groovy, kill the pigs." During the fight, he claimed his pajama top got pulled over his head, and he used it to parry off the blows from the icepick. He told the investigators that he was knocked unconscious in the living room. He woke up after the attackers had left and went into the bedroom, where he found Colette dead. He called in the stabbing to the operator and collapsed again after he covered her with his pajama top.

The army investigators did not believe his version of what happened at all. There were several pieces of evidence that didn't add up to the way he described the attack. There were no fibers from the pajama top found in the living room, where he claimed he used it to fight off blows from the icepick, but there were many fibers in the bedroom where Colette was found and in both of the girls' bedrooms. The living room was practically untouched. Pictures and Valentine's Day cards stood erect on tables in the area where Captain MacDonald claimed to have fought with three men for his life and the lives of his wife and daughters. The murder weapons were found outside the back door of the house and were items that had come from the house, and the tips of surgical gloves were found under the headboard by where the word "pig" had been written in blood. Also damning was a copy of *Esquire* magazine that contained an article describing the Manson murders, which were very similar to the scene the investigators found. By May 1, the army had formally charged Captain Jeffrey MacDonald with the murder of his wife and children.

During the army hearing, the attorney representing MacDonald brought forth the evidence that the crime scene had not been properly secured and evidence had been mishandled. He also brought forth information about a local police informant and drug addict, Helena Stoeckley, who claimed that she had been at the murders, but the police did not believe her. He was able to get the charges dismissed, and MacDonald was released from military service with an honorable discharge. He went back to New York and then moved to Long Beach, California, to work. After his release, his actions began to spark public interest in the case. He lived a carefree playboy lifestyle absent his family and even appeared on television joking and complaining about the investigation. Colette's stepfather, Freddie Kassab, who had helped MacDonald gain his freedom from the army and had been a supporter of him, began to turn against him and look into what he had been told by Jeffrey about the murders. He reviewed the army's investigation and found many inconsistencies with what the evidence showed and what he was being told by his son-in-law. He became convinced that he had assisted his stepdaughter's killer in gaining his freedom, and he filed a citizen's complaint through the United States Justice Department to reopen the case. After much persistence, a judge reopened the case, and a grand jury was assigned. The grand jury indicted MacDonald, and he was arrested in January 1975 but released on bail.

After many court proceedings to avoid going back to trial were swatted down by judges all the way up to the United States Supreme Court, the trial began in July 1979 in Raleigh. The prosecution presented a massive amount of evidence that there were no other people in the house on the night of the slayings, pointing out that although it was raining heavily outside, there was no water on the floors or walls in the house. Nor were there any wet or muddy footprints anywhere. The prosecutor even went so far as to wrap a similar pajama top around his hands and try to fend off strikes from an icepick in front of the jury, as MacDonald claimed to have done. The holes were jagged and torn, and he was cut on his hand. MacDonald had no injuries on his hands or arms, and the holes in the pajama top were perfectly round and lined up in a manner of the pajama top being laid flat when it was stabbed. Prosecutors presented evidence that MacDonald had been unfaithful to Colette and had many affairs, but despite everything, the weak point of their prosecution was the lack of a clear motive. The only real change that had occurred in the MacDonald family before the killing was the fact that Colette was once again pregnant when she was slain.

The jury did not believe the defense in its assertion that Helena Stoeckley was at the house the night of the murders and had taken part along with others. If MacDonald had heard screaming from his wife when he awoke to find Helena and three other men in the living room, then that would put the number of assailants at five. The two girls being murdered in their beds without fleeing or hiding would lead to the assumption of others being present. The house was just too small for there to be that many people in the house and not have more things out of place. They put MacDonald on the stand, and he denied committing the murders and emotionally expressed his regret that he had been unable to do more. The jury came back with a verdict of guilty of first-degree murder for the death of Kristen and second-degree murder for the deaths of Colette and Kimberly. He received a life sentence for each conviction. MacDonald has repeatedly appealed the verdict and has maintained his innocence to this very day. He refused parole for many years because he felt that it was admitting guilt but later did stand for and was denied parole in hopes that he could be released to live with his current wife, whom he married while in prison. He is eligible for parole again in 2020, but with the amount of physical evidence that exists, the chances are slim that he will ever be a free man again. Although no one but him will ever know what happened at 544 Castle Drive that rainy night, he will have the rest of his life to think about it.

Chapter 26
FRAGGING AT FORT BRAGG

F ort Bragg, located in the southern Piedmont of North Carolina, is the largest military base in the entire world. Established as an artillery training camp in 1918, the terrain and geography of the camp kept it alive during the post–World War I cuts that closed so many other facilities. During World War II, the camp became a hub for GIs training for the invasion of Europe. When the war was over, Fort Bragg became the permanent home to the famed Eighty-Second Airborne Division and has seen steady growth since then. Today, Fort Bragg is most famous as being the home of the Army Special Operations Command. Some of the finest young men and women the United States has ever produced have passed through the gates of Fort Bragg as soldiers. They have trained there and prepared to face combat in faraway places, but few, if any, would have ever thought that they would face enemy fire here at home.

On October 27, 1995, Colonel John Scroggins assembled 1,300 paratroopers at Towle Stadium for a brigade run to kick off, assuming the Readiness Brigade Mission, which meant that they had to be ready to deploy at a moment's notice to anywhere in the world. They were going to participate in a brigade run that morning to build camaraderie and prepare the soldiers for the training ahead. In the predawn darkness, the men stood at attention and saluted as reveille played over the speakers that were hung throughout the base. They began to file out of the stadium to form up for the run, not knowing they were being watched. When they had formed up in the stadium that morning, all were present and accounted for except for one: Sergeant William Kreutzer.

Fort Bragg in Fayetteville is a place where many heroes have trained to face enemies abroad. Few would have thought they would face death at the hands of one of their own here. *Author's collection.*

William Kreutzer joined the army in 1992, and by March of the next year, he had been assigned to the 325th Airborne Infantry Regiment of the 82nd Airborne. In January 1993, his unit was deployed to the Sinai Peninsula. He always found it hard to get along with other soldiers and was often on the receiving end of practical jokes and insults by his fellow troopers. He was known as being very uptight and would cry at any kind of negative reprimanding. In the Sinai, he broke down and cried, yelling at his superiors that he did not want to be there anymore and that he wanted to quit the unit. Other members of the unit began to report that he was fascinated by death and killing, often speaking about killing animals and humans. He began to be called "Crazy Kreutzer." He was finally referred to the unit's counselor, Captain (Dr.) Fong. He evaluated Kreutzer and found that he was very troubled and unable to cope with his anger and had considered suicide on several occasions, even putting a gun to his head or his chest at times. He took the findings to his supervisors, who removed Kreutzer's weapons and moved him to quarters with noncombat personnel, but Fong also reported to them that he felt Kreutzer was not a threat to anyone. After two weeks, Kreutzer returned to his unit and was back in the same situation that he was before. In October 1994, he attended the Primary Leadership Development Course and was promoted to sergeant.

The night before the brigade run that was scheduled for that foggy October morning, Kreutzer spoke to one of his former barrack mates and said he needed to talk to Dr. Fong again, that things were not all right with him. He also telephoned Specialist Burl Mays and informed him that he planned on firing on the run the next moving. Mays at first brushed it off, but when he arrived for formation at 5:00 a.m. the next morning, he told his superiors. They laughed and said Kreutzer was "too much of a pussy" to follow through with anything. Mays persisted in expressing that something was wrong, so they finally told him he could go and look for him in his room. Mays did not find him but did find that Kreutzer had made a will and left it there to be found. Realizing that he was not bluffing, he rushed to alert someone, but it was too late. As Mays was finding the will, William Kreutzer, dressed in battle fatigues, crept along the tree line near the stadium and took up position in a foxhole. He was armed with a Ruger .22 rifle, a PacWest Arms 5.56mm rifle and a 9mm semiautomatic pistol. As the soldiers broke ranks and moved to leave the stadium, he opened fire on them.

Kreutzer started firing with his .22 Ruger, a decision that might have saved the lives of many of his victims because of the smaller caliber. His first shot hit Chief Warrant Officer 2 Abraham Castillo in the neck. He fell to the ground, having taken his final step; the shot would make him into a quadriplegic for the rest of his life. The next shots were aimed at Sergeant Matthew Lewis, who was struck in the chest and back. Soldiers in the crowd knew the sound of live rounds because of the training they had gone through ever since their days in basic training. Some of the soldiers thought it was a planned training exercise, but when they started to see the casualties, everyone knew that the situation was deadly serious and real. They could not initially tell where the rounds were coming from and scattered in different directions to take cover. In all, sixteen soldiers were shot with the .22 rifle. When Kreutzer ran out of ammunition, he moved on to the 5.56mm rifle, which is the civilian equivalent to the military M16 rifle.

As Kreutzer switched rifles, Colonel Scroggins began to move toward the sound of the firing, hoping to outflank him and stop the carnage. His leadership staff followed him as he moved closer to Kreutzer. He spotted them and took aim. He shot Major Stephen Badger in the face, and he fell dead. Then he shot Major Guy Lo Faro in the stomach. Kreutzer began to retreat into the woods as they moved in on him. As his attention was focused on the approaching officers, he was tackled by some Special Forces soldiers who had been jogging nearby when they heard the sound of gunfire. They, with the help of the officers from Scroggins's group, subdued Kreutzer until the military police came and placed him under arrest. In all, eighteen soldiers had been shot, with one fatality.

William Kreutzer waived his rights and asked to speak with Dr. Fong. He had been reassigned, and Kreutzer was attended to by another doctor, who found him to be delusional and having very severe mental health issues. He was deemed fit to stand trial, found guilty and sentenced to death. Later he appealed and struck a plea bargain, and his sentence was reduced to life in prison. One of the factors of his life sentence was the sense of remorse that he showed to the court, but the life he took and the lives he destroyed cannot be restored by guilt. The injuries he caused cannot be undone. The blame for the tragedy has to be placed at the feet of the monster, William Kreutzer, but also at the antiquated system of recognizing and responding to mental health problems that the army had at the time. The hope of this sad event, as with any tragedy that occurs, is that others might be saved by lessons learned.

Chapter 27
SLEEPY TOWN TRAGEDY

Windsor has always been a sleepy little town in eastern North Carolina. Located in Bertie County, it started off as a small town that has managed to stay that way today. Chartered in the eighteenth century, Windsor was a hub for local farmers and also by the time of the Civil War had developed a successful brickmaking industry. On the Cashie River, which dumps into the Albemarle Sound, Windsor became a stop on the steamship lines that carried trade up and down the coast until the early twentieth century, when Windsor was connected to the vast web of railroads that crossed the state and nation. Throughout this modernization and growth, Windsor held out and maintained that small-town attitude. No one would have ever have thought that such a horrible thing could happen in such a peaceful place, but on a summer evening in 1993, that façade was shattered, as if the universe pointed to this little haven in rural North Carolina and said, "It can happen to you too."

Bud Cecil, the Be-Lo store manager, had closed the store on time at 6:00 p.m. on June 6, 1993. He had walked the store to make sure everything was ready for the next day, checking to make sure that everything was stocked, blocked and cleaned. While he did this, cashier Joyce Reason was counting down her till in the office. Cecil let in the cleaning crew of four in at 6:15 p.m. so they could get everything spic and span for the next day. Everything was the same as it had been every evening for the crew of the Be-Lo grocery store in Windsor. But this night was not like every other night. This night would change the way the townspeople thought about everything, including themselves, each other and their safety. The manager made small talk with the cleaning crew as the sound of Joyce counting her till back could be heard across the small store. She was ready to head home for the day—but she never finished counting the till or made it home that night.

From nowhere, a man appeared, holding a gun and shouting at everyone. "Do what I say and no one will get hurt" was the message he was giving them, and they were in no position to do anything but take him at his word. The stranger herded them up and moved them to the back of the store. He told them that he was a police officer who had been fired unfairly and was in need of money to get by. He assured them over and over that he was not a bad guy and they would be okay if they just complied with his commands. One by one, he forced Cecil to bind the others' hands behind their backs with duct tape. When he finished, the stranger bound Cecil's hands and led them into the meat cutting room and stacked them one on top of another in three piles. Lying on top of each other, they experienced the terror of the realization that he was not going to just take the money and go.

Once he delivered the last of the hostages to the cutting room and pushed them down onto the pile, he stepped back and admired his work. Their hearts beat loudly in their chests, and the people on the bottom could feel the beats on their backs. They were all afraid of what was going to happen next. The assailant walked around the room and began systematically shooting down into the people on top. After the third shot, his gun jammed, and he left the room for a moment. The survivors hoped he was gone, but he came right back into the room and began to roll each of the hostages onto their stomachs. He then grabbed a large butcher's knife from the cutting block and began to furiously stab and slash at his bound victims. He jammed the knife down into the back of one of his prey so hard it broke off into his back. He pulled the bloody broken knife out and walked out of the cutting room, which was covered in blood and filled with writhing bloody bodies and muffled cries for help.

The killer walked to the front of the store and took a canvas shopping bag from the cash register. He filled it with $3,000 and took the manager's keys with him. The killer slipped out of the door and disappeared into the night, never to be seen again. In the midst of the carnage in the cutting room, one of the cleaning crew, Tony Welch, who had been stacked under Joyce Reason, wiggled his way out from under her body and worked his hands out of the bloody duct tape that bound him. Although critically wounded, he crawled to the front of the store, not knowing if he was going to find himself again facing the killer, and called 911.

First responders were horrified at what they found when they entered the store. There was blood everywhere. Even a seasoned law enforcement officer in a big city could go his whole career and never see anything as horrific as what the small-town officers saw that night. Three of the victims were dead on the scene: store manager Bud Cecil, cashier Joyce Reason and Johnny Rankin, a member of the cleaning crew. Tony Welch, who was severely wounded but managed to crawl to the front to call for help, survived, along with two other members of the cleaning crew. One had also been severely wounded, and the other had miraculously been uninjured physically during the attack. Survivors of the attack described the killer as a black male between thirty and thirty-five years old with slanted eyes and a military-style haircut, with a unique narrow nose bridge that authorities thought could have been caused by a sports injury at some point. Every lead was followed in the days, months and years after the killings, but they all came up empty.

Today, Martin Community College is using the old Be-Lo building for classes. Despite a reward offered and the brutal nature of the crime, the killer has never surfaced. Law enforcement believed it was a lie that he was a former police officer who had been unfairly fired and that this was just

Crime scene photo taken outside of the Be-Lo store during the investigation of the savage attack by a stranger that left three people dead. *Courtesy of the Windsor Police Department.*

a way for him to calm the victims as he bound them. Officers reached out to departments all across the country regarding recently fired officers and found no one fitting the description of the murderer among them. The local authorities followed several leads, but they all ran into dead ends. The case remains unsolved to this day. Many of the young law enforcement officers who worked the case that hot June night have since retired, feeling a sense of disappointment that they were unable to collar the brutal murderer of their friends and neighbors in Windsor. All of the residents who lived there at the time no longer fool themselves to think that something like this cannot happen to them. Reality is now a resident in this sleepy little town, and somewhere out there is the cold-blooded killer who brought reality home.

Chapter 28
DEBBIE WOLFE

Debbie Wolfe was a blossoming flower at twenty-eight years old with her whole life ahead of her and everything on track for a great life. She worked as a nurse at the Veterans Hospital in Fayetteville, North Carolina, and she owned a cabin about four miles outside of town. She was the proud mom to two spoiled dogs named Mason and Morgan that she loved with all of her heart. Debbie was close with her mother and was liked by everyone who knew her. On the evening of Christmas Day 1985, she punched out of work after telling everybody merry Christmas and headed home. There was nothing to indicate to anyone that this would be the last time they saw her alive or that she was in danger, but Debbie was not long to remain in this world. Her light was soon to be snuffed out, and the lives of those who knew her were about to get darker.

At eight o'clock the next morning, she didn't show up for her shift. This sent red flags off for her coworkers because she rarely missed work, and never without calling in with a good reason. They tried several times to call her at home, but there was no answer. Finally, they called her mother, Jenny Edwards. Jenny was already getting a little worried because she had not heard from her since the previous day, which was very odd since it was Christmas and they were so close. She asked her friend Kevin Gordon to ride out to Debbie's house to check on her. When they arrived, Jenny immediately got a bad feeling. She noticed beer cans strewn across the yard and the dogs running lose. She knew that Debbie would never let the dogs run around like that, and she always kept the yard neat.

Since 1940, the Fayetteville VA Hospital has strived to fulfill Lincoln's promise "to care for him who shall have borne the battle, and for his widow, and his orphan." *Author's collection.*

They went into the house and found it was cluttered and Debbie's nurse uniform was thrown on the floor in the kitchen. Her mother felt a pit in her stomach grow as she walked through the house. Debbie always kept the house tidy and never threw things around. Kevin found Debbie's purse stuffed under her bed, and her mother noticed many other things out of place in odd ways. As she walked through the house, it seemed like Debbie did not even live there anymore. Everything was just wrong. She noticed the light was blinking on her answering machine and listened to the messages. One message in particular was very strange and caught her attention. It was an unfamiliar male voice on the tape that said, "Hey, Deb, missed you at work today. Just wondering how you're doing. If you're able to give me a call up here at the ward. I'm at the 822-7007. Or give me a call at home tonight. You've been out a lot of days; you made me worried when you missed another one. I just want to make sure you're okay. Bye." Jenny found the message disturbing because she didn't know the man's voice and because she knew that Debbie had not missed a lot of time from work. She searched the area around the cabin with Kevin, looking through the woods and around the pond behind the cabin, but could find nothing. Exasperated and worried, she called the police.

Captain Jack Watts from the Cumberland County Sheriff's Department showed up a short time later with a bloodhound. He spoke to Jenny and Kevin and searched the house and the property with the dog but also could find no trace of Debbie. He did not check in the pond because he did not have the equipment, and he told them that an extensive search could not be conducted until she had been missing for at least three days. Frustrated, Jenny went home and waited by the phone, hoping to hear from Debbie. Sadly, her phone did not ring. It was almost a week after Debbie had gone missing when the sheriff's department finally conducted an exhaustive search of the property. Still, when they were done, they had found nothing. Jenny was not satisfied with the results, so she had Kevin and another friend named Gordon Childress search the pond for any signs of Debbie. Gordon entered the pond that cold morning in his scuba gear and saw what he described as footprint indentions along the bottom of the pond. He followed them and found in the deepest end of the water a rusted fifty-five-gallon barrel with the body of Debbie Wolfe stuffed inside it. The sheriff's department was called back to the scene and recovered the body of Debbie Wolfe from the cold water of the pond.

Jenny Edwards was living a nightmare. Her beloved daughter had been taken from her, and she knew it, but the investigators saw it differently. After an autopsy was completed, it was ruled that the cause of death was undetermined, despite the indications of foul play, which included the fact that she had very little water in her lungs and her eyes and mouth were closed, which would not be consistent with a drowning death. Detectives felt that she might have been playing outside with her dogs and fallen into the pond or gone into the pond to rescue one of the dogs that she felt was in trouble and drowned. Jenny could not believe the results, but what was most puzzling to her was the issue of the barrel.

Kevin and Gordon had claimed to find her body in a barrel at the bottom of the pond. The sheriff's department claimed that when they reclaimed the body from the pond, there was no barrel. A barrel was never catalogued in evidence, but even a deputy who was part of the investigation later admitted it had been retrieved from the pond but not catalogued into evidence. Jenny, after being told of the barrel, remembered that Debbie had a fifty-five-gallon rusted burn barrel that she kept firewood in. When she went to look for it, all she found was a round indention in the ground. No barrel. The sheriff's department explained to the family that it could have been that when Gordon saw her under water, her jacket was ballooned out and might have appeared to be a barrel to him.

Further evidence began to surface pointing to foul play. When the coroner turned over the clothes that Debbie was wearing when she died to her mother, she was very surprised. She didn't recognize any of the clothes that Debbie had on. She was wearing brown corduroy pants that were too big on her. The bra she was wearing was three sizes too large, as were her shoes. She was wearing an army field jacket and a Pittsburgh Steelers T-shirt. The shoes were white Nike sneakers but had no mud on them—no indication that she had walked anywhere near the pond, much less into the mud and water. Later, after her body had been recovered, her uncle found her wool stocking cap on the opposite end of the pond on the bank. Also perplexing to Jenny was that a few days after her disappearance, her stepfather had come to the cabin to feed the dogs and found a short-sleeved nurse uniform shirt and some pantyhose on the floor in the kitchen. Jenny had not noticed this the day before, and when she spoke to Debbie's coworkers, they told her that she had been wearing a long-sleeved shirt the last day she worked. They remembered specifically because someone had spilled coffee on her sleeve accidentally.

The detectives interviewed several people in regard to her death even though it was ruled an undetermined death. There were several employees and volunteers at the hospital who had expressed interest in Debbie but

When Debbie Wolfe left work on Christmas Eve 1985, she had no idea that she would never return. *Author's collection.*

had been rebuffed. None of the leads went anywhere. The man who had left the message was a patient at the hospital, and he was questioned. He refused to take a polygraph, but he had an alibi for his whereabouts the night of her disappearance. Jenny Edwards has never given up on finding the truth about what happened to her daughter that Christmas in 1985. There were so many red flags in her death that it just seems beyond the realm of possibility that law enforcement could have come to the conclusion that it was not due to foul play. Still today, many people question the investigation of her death and the manner in which evidence was collected and interpreted. The questions hang in the air like fog to this day around the cabin and pond outside Fayetteville—questions that may never be answered, with the biggest question to those who loved Debbie always being "Why?"

Chapter 29
NELL CROPSEY

In 1898, the Cropsey family moved from Brooklyn, New York, to Elizabeth City, North Carolina, on the green waters of the Pasquotank River to farm. Elizabeth City was once a major port in the New World where tall sailing ships brought goods and people from far away in the Old World. It was a move that William Cropsey would have never thought would have led to so much tragedy and hurt for his family. His youngest daughter, Nell, was a beautiful girl and soon became the belle of the town. The former sheriff's son, Jim Wilcox—who was a very strange fellow, as most said around town—courted her. After three years of courting, Nell had become frustrated by his lack of initiative and his reluctance to ask her to marry him. She had become very flirty with other young men in town in the hopes of driving Jim to marriage through jealousy. Being so pretty and from a good family, it seemed Nell could have had most any young man in Elizabeth City, but she wanted Jim.

On the evening of November 20, 1901, Jim came to the Cropsey house to visit with Nell. There they had an argument that made the family feel awkward all throughout the house. They could hear yelling and sobbing, but no one wanted to get involved in the lovers' quarrel. Lately, they had been quarreling mostly over Jim's lack of commitment to the relationship. By the end of the night though, it seemed that they had made up, and the gentle murmurs the family heard later in the night assured them that the trouble in paradise had passed. Around eleven o'clock, Nell walked out on the front porch with Jim to say goodnight. She was never seen again.

Her family all assumed she had tarried on the porch with Jim and gone to bed, but Jim's story was different. He maintained that he left her crying on the porch because they were still fighting, and he walked home. Nell's sister Ollie heard a bang out back sometime after Nell had walked Jim out. She checked it out and found that the back screen door was damaged, but she could not see anything that might have caused the damage. When she returned upstairs, she looked into Nell's room to see if she was there, but her bed was empty. Assuming she was still talking to Jim, considering the fight they had that night, she went back to bed. She and the rest of the family were awakened sometime later by shouts from a neighbor saying someone was trying to steal one of their pigs. William ran downstairs to engage the thief, with his family trailing behind him to catch the action. They found the front door wide open but no pig thief. It was at this moment, though, that they first noticed the absence of Nell.

They checked her room and outside, calling her name in the darkness, but to no avail. She was gone. Dawn brought the awakening of the town and an all-hands-on-deck search for the young lady. Men gathered and began looking around in the neighborhoods and surrounding woods. When they could find no trace of her, they got their boats and took to the river, looking up and down the shore and scanning the water. The town police immediately spoke with Jim and found his story lacking. He was arrested and held in the town jail while the townspeople searched and became more and more incensed at the man they were confident had done something to this beautiful girl. He waited, and they searched, and still no Nell.

Searches in town and the woods produced nothing. Up and down the river, there was not a sign of her. They dragged the river by Elizabeth City and even far downstream with no results. Cannons were fired from ships across the river in hopes that the concussion of the blast would bring up her body from the depths, but nothing was working. Nell's mother sat in the highest room in the Cropsey house looking out the window at the river hoping to see a sign of her daughter being found—hopefully alive somehow. Nell had been missing for thirty-seven days when her mother climbed the stairs and looked once more out on the river. There she saw a commotion on the water. Boats were converging on a spot on the river. Her heart sunk because she knew that Nell had been found and that she was gone.

A mob began to form as word got around Elizabeth City of the discovery of Nell's body. They marched to the jail and demanded the release of Jim Wilcox with intentions of lynching him. The local police had to call for help from the governor, who sent out a naval reserve unit to break up the crowd and secure the jail so that Wilcox could stand trial. He made it to trial and was found guilty of murder, but because of the attempted lynching and the other activities that had taken place during the trial in the media and in the courtroom, the North Carolina Supreme Court declared a mistrial and sent Wilcox back to trial again. In his second trial, he was again found guilty but this time of second-degree murder. He stayed in prison until 1920, when Governor Thomas Bickett pardoned him. He maintained his innocence throughout his imprisonment and the rest of his life. In 1932, he committed suicide, having never publicly spoken about the incidents leading to his conviction.

Even though Jim Wilcox was convicted twice of the murder of Nell Cropsey, there has been a fog of mystery and uncertainty still to this day around her death. There were several strange occurrences that have never been explained. First there was the letter. Just a few days before her body was discovered, the Cropsey family received a letter postmarked from New York. The letter contained a detailed account of the murder of Nell. According to the letter, Nell had come upon a thief after Jim left that night, and he had killed her by striking her with a stick to the head. He then took her body down to the river, stole a boat and dumped her body in the river. There was also a map that marked the spot where she was dumped, which was close to the area she was found a few days later. The authorities were never able to authenticate the letter or trace it back to its origins.

The other strange thing about her death was that when the body was taken out of the Pasquotank River after thirty-seven days of a full effort to find her, she was very well preserved. She had not been molested by any wildlife or washed a far distance away. Most expected that when they found her body, the turtles and fish would have done their work on her, but she remained in death a beautiful young lady just as in life. Also, strangely, she did not have water in her lungs when they performed an autopsy on her body. It appeared that she had been killed by a trauma to her head. Corresponding to this was an excessively high ice bill at the Cropsey house during the month that she had been missing. Many speculated that her father, William, had something to do with her death and had kept her body preserved in the house until he was able to dispose of it in the river at a later time. There is no information that would point to a motive by her father or any other family members though. Whatever happened to Nell Cropsey will most definitely remain a mystery, but one thing is for certain. A young life was taken from this world far too soon, and her light was never allowed to shine over the course of the long life she deserved.

Chapter 30
DEATH OF THE FORT FISHER HERMIT

In the same manner that tourists come to the North Carolina coast to see the wild horses of Corolla or the historic lighthouses at Ocracoke and Hatteras, people once ventured through the dunes and beach grass at Fort Fisher to meet the hermit. Tanned, shirtless and in a hat woven from grass, he could be found fishing or working on something around the old abandoned army bunker he called home. Always willing to stop and impart wisdom or take photos with tourists, he was an attraction all by himself. His salt-and-pepper beard made him look like Hemingway, and he lived a life that many wished they were brave enough to live. Many had met him, but few knew who this solitary man truly was.

Robert E. Harrill was born in Gaffney, South Carolina, in the winter of 1893. When he was a small boy, his mother died and his father remarried. Robert felt abused by his stepmother and even at a young age sought solace in the woods around their home. When she would yell at him or scold him, he would retreat among the pines and get lost in nature until he had to return to reality. His father moved the family to Shelby, North Carolina, in pursuit of work, and it was there that Robert first began to visit Carolina Beach. He married Kate Hamrick and over the next few decades had five children and several jobs. He tried but just couldn't seem to find his place in the world, and Kate was often left holding the bag, taking care of Robert and the children with help from her parents.

In 1955, Kate petitioned for divorce from Harrill, and her parents later had him committed involuntarily to the Broughton Mental Hospital in

Morgantown, North Carolina, due to what they viewed as his instability. Robert chafed at the restraints at the hospital and made a key out of a spoon. After lights out, he opened the door and just walked out, promising to find true freedom. He hitchhiked all the way to Carolina Beach and found refuge in the dunes and the marshlands. His first attempt at setting up residence there was not successful, and he was arrested by the sheriff's department and taken back to Shelby. Undeterred, he returned the following summer to take up permanent residence among the sand crabs and scrub oaks. He found an old army artillery bunker that had been built during the Second World War but had been abandoned a decade before. He learned to harvest oysters and mussels and to fish. He learned basic survival skills but also began to subsist on many of the things that tourists would bring him. People brought him clothes and food and also gave him money for pictures and sometimes just to help him out.

He was not a true hermit in every sense of the word. Harrill wanted to leave the rat race and check out from society, but he still loved the company of others. He began to entertain and to have people constantly at his camp. At one point, he was the most popular attraction in North Carolina, followed by the battleship USS *North Carolina* in Wilmington just down the road. He recited poetry, grew vegetables and delighted in showing tourists how he lived. People began leaving donations for him, and many of the locals would often come down to the beach to check on him and bring him supplies. There are many pictures of the hermit existing today because he was quick to offer to pose for photos for a small fee. Robert Harrill found his happy place in life and peace, but just as many loved to come and spend time with him and take pictures, others sought to harass and hurt him.

At first, even the local authorities harassed him and viewed him as a vagrant and a trespasser. Robert was a hippie about a decade before people even knew what that was. He preached about slowing down and living a peaceful life centered on common sense. Despite his unthreatening presence, he often found himself fighting off drunken tourists and locals who had come to his bunker to have a go at him. There was nowhere to run for the hermit. When the bad people came, he just did the best that he could to fight them off and returned to his bunker oftentimes with a bloody nose or a black eye. Many people came to rob him, thinking that he had some hidden fortune from years of collecting change from tourists, although there is no evidence of such a treasure.

Harrill crossed many people just with his presence there on the salt marsh. The land had been formed because of shoaling in the area, and

Robert Harrill spent the last sixteen years of his life among the dunes and scrub oaks of Carolina Beach as the Fort Fisher Hermit. *Courtesy of WRAL News.*

there was no claim to the land he lived on. The state wanted him gone because improvements were being made to Fort Fisher Historic Site and it felt that his presence would degrade the progress. The federal government wanted Harrill gone because of his proximity to the Sunny Point Arsenal that was across the river. There was also a housing development that found the Hermit to be a nuisance. While drawing up plans for the community, the builders were shocked to find him living right in the middle of phase one and phase two of their subdivision plans. But no matter who tried to pry the Hermit out, he always seemed to find a way to stay.

On a Sunday morning in 1972, some local teenagers decided to go down to the salt marsh and bring the Hermit some cigarettes. When they arrived at the bunker, they called for him, but there was an eerie silence, with only the sound of the wind blowing through the dunes. They approached the bunker and looked inside. Harrill was lying on his back with his feet close to the door. Jeff Barbour reached out and pulled the Hermit's big toe in hopes of waking him up, but when he touched the toe, it felt cold and lifeless. He stepped back and knew the Hermit was dead. The boys struck out back to the car and rushed back to town, where they reported the death to the police. When the police checked the bunker, they saw that the boys were telling the truth. Robert Harrill, the Hermit of Fort Fisher, was dead.

A small crowd gathered around the bunker as the police investigated. The Hermit was covered in sand and mud. He had sand in his pockets and even in his hair. He had several small cuts on his legs and on his head. Outside the bunker there were tire tracks and drag marks. There appeared to be signs of a struggle in the sand around the bunker and on the trail leading through the salt marsh down to the water. A sleeping bag and one of the Hermit's shoes were found in the marsh off the trail. It appeared to some of the local police that the Hermit had been attacked at his bunker and dragged inside his sleeping bag through the marsh and down to the ocean, probably by people who were looking to have some fun at his expense or even people who might have been trying to rob him. They felt that he had a heart attack sometime during the assault and died. The killers then threw his body into the bunker and drove away from their deed.

Although there was an element of the local police that felt there was foul play involved, the case was closed by higher authorities, probably because they felt that they really had no one to answer to for the death of the Hermit. Although he was loved and known by thousands, he was still an

The World War II bunker where the Fort Fisher Hermit lived still stands today. *Author's collection.*

old man who was alone in this world. He was estranged from his family and had just recently reconnected with them a few years before. The cost of an in-depth investigation for the Hermit was not justified, and there was very little evidence that could have possibly led back to anyone. He came into contact with so many people from all around the country that the chances of tracing any evidence were small. His death will remain unsolved because of the lack of leads and the amount of time that has passed. One thing is for certain though: the Hermit of Fort Fisher has been gone for many decades now, but he has not been forgotten and will always be part of North Carolina's history and lore.

SELECTED BIBLIOGRAPHY

Books

Bledsoe, Jerry. *Before He Wakes: A True Story of Money, Marriage, Sex, and Murder*. New York: Penguin Books, 1994.

———. *Blood Games*. New York: Penguin Books, 1991.

Casstevens, Frances H. *Death in North Carolina's Piedmont: Tales of Murder, Suicide and Causes Unknown*. Charleston, SC: The History Press, 2006.

Long-Wilgus, Eleanor R. *Naomi Wise: Creation, Re-Creation, and Continuity in an American Ballad Tradition*. Chapel Hill, NC, 2003.

McGinniss, Joe. *Cruel Doubt*. New York: Simon & Schuster, 1991.

———. *Fatal Vision*. New York: G.P. Putnam's Sons, 1983.

The North Carolina Tragedy: Trial of the Rev. Geo. W. Carawan, Baptist Preacher. New York: printed for the proprietor, 1854.

Paludan, Phillip Shaw. *Victims: A True Story of the Civil War*. Knoxville: University of Tennessee Press, 2004.

Pickler, Fred, and Daniel Ray Norris. *The Reluctant Hermit of Fort Fisher*. Carolina Beach, NC: SlapDash Publishing, 2014.

Pinsky, Mark I. *Met Her on the Mountain: A Forty Year Quest to Solve the Appalachian Cold-Case Murder of Nancy Morgan*. Winston-Salem, NC: John F. Blair Publishing, 2013.

Simpson, Bland. *The Mystery of Beautiful Nell Cropsey: A Nonfiction Novel*. Chapel Hill: University of North Carolina Press, 1993.

Wellman, Manly Wade. *Dead and Gone*. Chapel Hill: University of North Carolina, 1980.

Wilhelm, Robert. *The Bloody Century: True Tales of Murder in 19th Century America*. N.p.: Night Stick Press, 2014.

Young, Perry Deane. *The Untold Story of Frankie Silver: Was She Unjustly Hanged?* Lincoln, NE: iUniverse, 2005.

Periodicals

Asheville Citizen Times
Charlotte Observer
Daily Tar Heel
Durham Herald-Sun
Fayetteville Observer
Greensboro News and Record
Raleigh News and Observer
Roanoke-Chowan News Herald
Winston-Salem Journal

Selected Websites

Godwin, Maurice. "30 Years Later, Murder of Nurse Found in Rural Fayetteville, NC Pond Is Still Shrouded in Mystery." www.drmauricegodwin.com.

Hunt, Max. "Blood in the Valley: The Shelton Laurel Massacre's Haunting Legacy." Mountain Xpress, January 28, 2016. mountainx.com.

Murder by Gaslight. www.murderbygaslight.com.

INDEX

ABOUT THE AUTHOR

Rick Jackson is a native North Carolinian who grew up in Durham and now lives with his family in Wake Forest, just outside Raleigh. He currently teaches business and economic courses to high school students after spending many years in banking and finance in various positions. He has always had a passion for history and the stories of the people who lived it. He holds a bachelor's degree in history from Campbell University and an MBA from the University of Mount Olive. Rick enjoys traveling around North Carolina with his wife, Meghan, and their three children, Savannah, Ricky and Charlotte. Rick's first book, *Ghosts of the Triangle*, was written with his brother, William Jackson, and was also published by The History Press.

Visit us at
www.historypress.com
....